AF539225

THE ROLI GUIDE TO
Shopping
in Mumbai

THE ROLI GUIDE TO

MALLIKA AGARWALLA
SHRUTI RATHI

To our parents:

Rajendra and Minakshi Saraf
Dipak and Vibha Agarwalla

Who have dressed us up for life.

Lotus Collection

First published in 2005
The Lotus Collection
An imprint of Roli Books Pvt. Ltd.
M-75, G.K. II Market, New Delhi 110 048
Phones: ++91 (011) 2921 2271, 2921 2782, 2921 0886
Fax: ++91 (011) 2921 7185 E-mail: roli@vsnl.com
Website: rolibooks.com

Also at Varanasi, Bangalore, Jaipur and the Netherlands

Cover design: Arati Subramanyam
Layout design: Narendra Shahi

ISBN: 81-7436-411-0
Rs. 195

Typeset in Bliss-Light by Roli Books Pvt. Ltd.

Printed at Tan Prints (India) Pvt. Ltd. Jhajjar (Haryana)

CONTENTS

ACKNOWLEDGEMENTS

Thanks to our family and friends for their encouragement, belief and patience.
And a special thanks to each of the following, who helped in the compilation of the book:
Manjri Agarwal, Vibha Agarwalla, Archana Bajaj, Vivek Kagzi
and Gaurav Singhania.

This guide would not have been possible without all of your help and support.

DISCLAIMER

The only thing constant in life is change; thus in time, shops close, new ones open and current ones reinvent themselves. Although every effort has been made to ensure the accuracy of the information herein, the publishers and authors, make no claims to or accept any liabilities for any misrepresentation contained in the book. Factual information is correct to the best of our knowledge at the time of compilation, while the reviews are based on personal opinions of the authors.

INTRODUCTION

Hello Shoppers,

Shining on the glitterati and the Bollywood stars, Mumbai's sun savours an abounding expanse of shopping retreats. With no mentor to guide hapless shopoholics as to where to go next, we decided to bring to light, the most precious of these jewels that adorn our city. The Roli Guide to Shopping in Mumbai, the city's first and only fashion guide of clothing, accessory and lifestyle stores welcomes you to sashay into Mumbai's up-market fashion boutiques and out-of-the-way treasure houses.

This debut edition of The Roli Guide to Shopping in Mumbai provides you with all the insider secrets you need, to look and feel fab, whether it is for a 'black-tie' event or a girlie 'dim-sum' lunch. The list of lifestyle stores included in the book have also been especially handpicked by us to radiate some of the best of the luxury offerings available in tinsel town. We have covered over 500 shopping destinations ranging from the high-streets of south Mumbai to the peripherals of the suburbs. This guide shows visitors where to begin and Mumbai-ites where to go next. If you want rock-star ripped jeans or one of a kind coffee cups we show you where to glow.

We have trekked up every uprising mall and tromped down every street market to invite the best shops to be a part of The Roli Guide to Shopping in Mumbai. We tell you what the stores are about, the products they entail, their target customers and price ranges. Also included are addresses, phone numbers and opening hours, along with parking facilities offered, for your convenience. All the stores have been categorized and cross-referenced by location and genre, while the ones that have appealed to us, have been especially highlighted (✺). Enlightening you with what is sassy, sensual, sober, sporty, or even simply simple, we hope to have been as accurate as possible. Please let us know if you feel otherwise (massfashion@gmail.com).

To add sugar to the already sweet and pomp to the already pompous, we have included two maps which help you find your way around the city. The Roli Guide to Shopping in Mumbai is completed with the 'fashion lingo' used throughout the book, along with size conversion charts to make sure you get the right size and fit.

So fasten your seat belts, rev up your credit cards and jet-set for your one and only guided shopping spree!

MALLIKA AND SHRUTI

Mogra

Rs 150- 1,20,000

A classy showroom with faux fur carpets, Mogra believes in encouraging new talent. With its primary focus on Indian and western prêt collections, the shop also flaunts some outstanding miscellanea in footwear, stoles and funky handbags. Showcased at the store's rear end is a small but truly exquisite collection of trendy imitation and real jewellery, making this modish store an inviting fashion aphrodisiac.

No. 10 Quorum,
1st floor,
High Street Phoenix,
462 Senapati Bapat Marg,
Lower Parel,
Mumbai 400 013
Ph. 91 22 3097 1300/30

mograstyle@yahoo.co.in

DAILY 11-8.30

Mont Blanc

Rs 4,000 onwards

This world-renowned brand carries classy accessories such as leather belts, wallets, silver cuff links, eyewear and signature pens. The perfect place to shop for a 'black-tie' event, or a family heirloom, Mont Blanc can make a gift truly memorable through personalized inscription. Boasting of superlative craftsmanship, the shop's accessories are a definite style statement, while ladies can look swish in the brand's latest collection of leather wallets and accessories.

The Taj Mahal Hotel
Apollo Bunder
Mumbai 400 001
Ph. 91 22 22852151

anna@entrackonline.com
www.montblanc.com

DAILY 10-10

Morgan

Rs 1,500 onwards

All you fashion-struck chicas, listen up. Morgan brings fashion to India all the way from Paris just for you. From casual t-shirts, to sophisticated formal outfits, everything here comes in tight cuts and bright colours, and of course, lots and lots of attitude. Mostly made with Lycra, the clothes cling on to your body for dear life, and only ask to be strutted around and admired in response. So for a groovy look, make sure you vroom in!

The Courtyard
41/44 Minoo Desai Marg, Colaba
Mumbai 400 005
Ph. 91 22 5638 5460/61
MAP1 80

morgan@apgroupindia.com

DAILY 10-8.30

Alphabetical Listing by Store Name

Price Range: From the lowest to the highest

Clothes, Handbags, Footwear & Jewellery available

Store Hours

Best Pick

Handbags & Leather accessories

Parking Facilities

Website

Who it is for: Men, Women or Children

Credit Card Accepted

Telephone Numbers

Map Reference

Email

KEY

- Credit Cards Accepted
- No Credit Cards Accepted
- Parking Available
- No Parking Available
- Valet Parking
- Men's
- Women's
- Children's
- Clothes
- Jewellery
- Handbags and Leather Accessories
- Footwear
- Lifestyle
- Departmental Stores

FASHION LINGO

AMBI/ KAIRI: A green mango, normally illustrated as a paisley print.

ANGRAKHA: Literally meaning 'that which protects or covers the limbs'. This is a long, full-sleeved outerwear for men worn in varying lengths. Usually open at the chest and tied in front, with an inner flap or parda covering the chest.

AVANT-GARDE: Innovative or forward-thinking design — often implies erotic or startling when used with respect to fashion. Literally meaning "advance guard" in French.

BAAGH PRINT: Literally, "a garden print". A floral motif used in Indian textile design that may be rendered as a flowering plant with a curling bud at the top or simply a floral pattern designed within the form of the plant.

BADLA: Flat metallic wire (sometimes silver-gilt) used in brocading and embroidery that is mostly hammered on to the fabrics by craftsmen.

BANARSI: A special kind of weaving carried out by skilled artisans in Banaras (Varanasi). The work usually speaks of femininity and grace.

BANDHANI/ BANDHEJ: Cloth patterned by tie-and-dye method. The designs are formed by tying small spots/knots very tightly with thread to protect the cloth from dying all over. Especially popular in Rajasthan and Gujarat, these garments are worn during the Navratri or Dandiya Festival native to Gujarat.

BARATI: Members included in the bridegroom's marriage procession.

BATWA: A clutch purse used by ladies.

BINDI/ TIKKI: An auspicious, decorative dot worn by Indian women on the middle of their foreheads. Traditionally made of a red powder called 'kum-kum'.

CHAND-TARA: Literally, "moon and star", a pattern often-used on Indian textiles.

CHAPPAL: The Indian world for a flat open sandal.

CHIKAN KARI: Embroidery in white cotton threads adorns fine cotton fabrics, like, muslin so that the inside of the embroidery can show. Several techniques in chikan-kari are known, while Lucknow's & Kotwara District are famous centres for fine workmanship.

CHOLI: Women's close-fitting, bodice-like upper garment worn with either a sari or skirt. The garment is short sleeved, leaves the midriff bare, and can be worn in various styles: with back covering or without, fastened with strings or extended cloth-pieces, with shaped breast-pieces or flat, etc.

CHURIDAR: A tight-fitting trouser with bangle-like gathers or wrinkles near the ankles.

COUTURE: Design and making of fashion garments.

DHAKAI: Dhakai muslin originating from East Bengal has now lost its legendary fineness; but it continues as Jamdani, with beautiful extra weft decorations on a fine surfaces.

DHOTI: A traditional Indian dress for the lower part of the male body, this garment consists of a piece of unstitched cloth, draped over the hips and legs.

DORI-WORK: Thread-work embroidery.

DUPATTA: A large piece of cloth loosely draped by women over the upper parts of their bodies.

GADWAL: These are real zari saris, woven with silk-zari borders and a cotton background. Originating from Andhra Pradesh and washed to an astounding softness, these saris are ideal for daily wear.

GARA: Influenced by Chinese and Persian cultures, the Gara embroidery includes bird, flower and fruit motifs. The modern versions of the Gara however, incorporate traditional motifs with Swarovski crystal and touches of gold and silver interweaving.

GHAGHRA: Indian skirts, usually with a lot of flare. The simple ghaghras have only one vertical seam, which turns the cloth or ghaghra-pata into a tube, and fastened with a drawstring passing at the waist. Flared ghaghras are made up of, several triangular gored pieces or 'kalis' stitched together, to be called a 'kalidar'.

GOTA: A narrow ribbon made of gold or silver thread.

GUNJEE: A sleeveless vest usually in cotton.

HAUTE COUTURE: French word used in the fashion industry to describe original styles and extremely fine designs, tailored on expensive fabrics. Designs which are shown in seasonal collections twice a year- spring/summer and fall/winter.

IKAT: Originating from the Indonesian mengikat, 'to tie' or 'to bind'. It is a resist-dye process in which designs are impressed in the warp or weft yarns by tying small bundles of yarn with palm-leaf strips to prevent from colouration.

JADAO/JADTAR: Ethnic Indian jewellery set in gold with uncut diamonds and stones.

JAMA: Full-sleeved outerwear for men, greatly popular at the Mughal and Rajput courts and worn well into the 19th century. Literally meaning a garment, robe, or coat.

JAMDANI: Fine cotton muslin with a floral pattern brocaded on thick soft cotton. Varanasi (Banaras) is a famous centre for the production of fine jamdani work.

JHUMKA: Long, ornate dangling Indian earrings.

JOOTIS: Earlier used as a modest Indian foot accessory, the jooti has now reinvented itself. Embellished with seed pearls, sequence etc., the shoe fuses the East and West fashions and can therefore be worn with Western clothes as well.

JUDA PIN: A special kind of pin designed to hold a hair-bun.

KADA: An ornate traditional bangle.

KAFTAN: A long gown with sleeves reaching below the hands; generally fastened by a belt or sash.

KALAMKARI: Originating from the Persian word 'Kalam' meaning pen and 'kari' meaning work, it is a kind of fabric painting wherein traditionally, the kalam is dipped in the ink and the wool fabric is pressed while applying the paint on the fabric.

KALIRA: Light ornaments of beaten silver and gold called kalira, are tied to the bangles of the bride's chura.

KAMEEZ: A loose jacket worn traditionally with baggy trousers and a scarf by the women of Punjab. Men traditionally wear a similar simplified version of this garment, with Churidar, Lungi or Dhoti bottoms.

KANGAN: A hindi term for bracelet.

KANJIVARAMS: These silk saris are famous as the finest and most beautiful ones in the world. Passed on from generations, the garments are made from worms bred purely on mulberry, and the end products are spectacularly adorned with zari.

KHADI: Hand-spun, woven cloth made of 'khaddar'.

KITSCH: Loud colours and vibrant designs take inspiration from flea markets, truck art, etc. A Common-place thing taken to the pedestal of art.

KOLHAPURI: These chappals made by Kolhapur artisans are open-cut and are designed to be slipped-on. Soft and comfortable, these leather wears last long, due to their high quality and fine workmanship.

KORA: Originating from Banaras, the Kora silk is blended with lesser yarns. Its fabric is tightly woven, and has a sheen to it, which though not unattractive, is not preferred by people living in sultry climates.

KUNDAN: Uncut diamonds, used in making traditional Jadtar sets.

KURTA: A moderately loose-fitting garment, usually with a round neck, of knee-length, and with slits running along the side hems.

KURTI: Open under the throat, this shirt-like garment has most of the features of a kurta, except that it is a little shorter and only reaches up to the hip.

LAC: A resinous secretion of an insect used to make shellac. Used to make bangles in India.

LEHENGA: A kind of flared skirt worn generally with a dupatta.

LEHERIYA: A kind of fabric dying from the regions of Rajasthan and Gujarat, in oblique wave-like designs.

LUNGI: A one-piece cloth, worn by men as a long straight skirt.

MAANG-TIKKA: An ornament worn along the parting of the hair and on the middle of the head.

MADHUBANI: A famous kind of Indian art practised by the women of Madhubani and the surrounding area of Mithila. Madhubani paintings are folk art and thus are less refined.

MEHENDI: Henna applied on hands by women as a symbol of festivities. Conventionally applied on a bride before her wedding.

MOJRIS: These are traditionally handcrafted slippers and shoes from Rajasthan, usually worn with ethnic Indian outfits.

MUKAISH: Tiny disks of beaten silver or gold are decoratively sown onto delicate fabrics to give the fabrics a shimmering look.

NAKA-TIKKI: A small stud worn on the nose.

PALLOO: The hanging end of a sari.

PASHMINA: Popularly known as cashmere, Pashmina is a precious fibre gathered from high Himalayan goats, Chayngra, in Nepal. The softest wool found in nature, it is known for its exotic silky texture, lightness and warmth.

PATHANI: A kind of jacket originally worn by the people from the region of Pathan.

PATOLA: The Patola of Patan is a unique fabric of Gujarat, the striking colourful geometrical patterns are made of hand-woven and silken yarns. Its tie and weave method result in identical patterns on both sides of the fabric, involving complicated calculations related to the proposed designs.

PATTI: Kind of fabric trimmings stitched on for embellishments.

PAYAL: A hindi word for anklet, usually in silver.

PHULKARI: Flower-patterned embroidery used greatly by women in the Punjab for head-veils and other garment-pieces.

POLYSONIC: A blend of polyester and Rayon, known for its crease-resistance, shape retention and requirement of minimum care.

PONCHO-TOP: A traditional South American cloak; consisting of a rectangular piece of fabric, with a slit in the middle, for the head.

PRÊT-À-PORTER: Literally means 'ready-to-wear' in French – implies clothes that you can take or wear straight out of the shop.

PYJAMA: Trouser-like garment to cover the lower part of the body. Can be worn in many cuts and shapes, with variation in girth, length, and tightness.

RESHAM: A form of fine-needled embroidery done with silk thread by skilful workers.

SALWAR: A pyjama-like garment, baggy and wide at the top, and not so tight around the legs and ankles, worn mostly by women to cover the lower half of their bodies.

SARI: A traditional outfit worn by Indian women, this garment is a single piece of cloth, usually six yards long and a little more than one meter wide. Wrapped around the body, the cloth is pleated in the front, while the rest of it, is thrown over one shoulder and made to hang at the back.

SHERWANI: A man's knee-length coat, worn close to the body and opening in the front, with button-fastenings. Also called the achkan in Hyde rabad.

SHRINGAR: An Indian term to adorn oneself.

ZARDOZI WORK: A kind of work in which gold or silver metal threads are sewn on fabrics like satin or velvet, in order to give the appearance of true embroidery work on them.

ZARI: Metallic threads twisted over cottons or silks, for brocading.

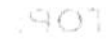

ALPHABETICAL DIRECTORY

BEST PICKS

Aadi's

Rs. 40- 7,000

A refreshing respite in the hoi polloi of the area, Aadi's attractive display of imitation jadao sets, antique looking silver and gold plated kundan and coloured stone sets add music to the mannequins; while 1 gram gold jewellery, kadas with jhumkas, and crystal nail tattoos adorn the textured walls. Offering a fine collection of ethnic accessories, this shop is a good destination when fixing an outfit for your best friends' wedding.

16 Patel Building
Ganesh Gavde Road
Near Swaminarayan
Mandir
Mulund (W)
Mumbai 400 080
Ph. 91 22 2590 2619
MAP1 2

DAILY 10-9 (Thurs closed)

Aakanksha

Rs. 1,000 onwards

If you have no time or inclination to search for the perfect Indian ensemble, Aakanksha might be your final resort. A convenient shopping option with a huge range of saris and salwar kameez to choose from, the shop's embroidered works come in various forms, updated with the latest trends. Beaded stoles and art jewellery available here also deserve to be noticed.

6 Vaishali Shopping
Centre,
V.M. Road,
Vile Parle (W),
Mumbai 400 049
Ph. 91 22 2611 7622/
2614 4452, MAP1 3

DAILY 9.30-8.30

Aari

Rs 2,400- 1,00,000

'The Designer Trousseau' boutique presents traditional lehengas and embroidered saris to its 'brides-to-be' customers. Garments are embellished with chikan kari and Kolkata handwork, while the colour palette used by the designers there, celebrate the hues of the forthcoming season. Overall, an up-to-date store with up-there prices.

5 Warden Court,
August Kranti Marg,
Mumbai 400 036
Ph. 91 22 3096 5732

DAILY 11-7 (Sun closed)

Abhushan

Rs 200- 5,000

More of a stopover attraction than a destination in its own right, Abhushan displays a range of delicate silver bangles and pendants. A fairly new entrant to the string of jewellery shops in the area, this alcove also stocks moderately heavy antique jewellery sets studded with kundan and zircons. Do drop by this small and modest shop if you are in the neighbourhood.

134 /C
Sikka Nagar
V.P. Road
Mumbai 400 004
Ph. 91 22 2388 2733

DAILY 11-7 (Sun closed)

Abracadabra

Rs 250 onwards

Walk into this and other tempting household whimsical store for loots full of household goodies. Candle stands, frames cushions and accessories all available here. The furniture selection includes sofas, coffee tables and wine units. You can also browse and place orders from the catalogues available.

DAILY 11-8

Junction of 8th and
Linking Road
Diagonally Opp Tanishq
Showroom
Khar (W)
Mumbai 400 052
Ph. 91 22 2605 7920/22
MAP1 4

Abraham & Thakore

Rs 1,200- 4,000

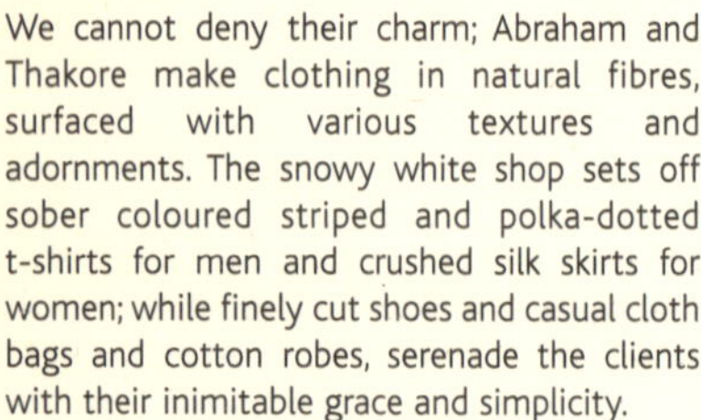

We cannot deny their charm; Abraham and Thakore make clothing in natural fibres, surfaced with various textures and adornments. The snowy white shop sets off sober coloured striped and polka-dotted t-shirts for men and crushed silk skirts for women; while finely cut shoes and casual cloth bags and cotton robes, serenade the clients with their inimitable grace and simplicity.

abrahamandthakore@vsnl.com
www.abrahamandthakore.com

DAILY 10.30-8 (Sun closed)

The Courtyard
15, S.P Centre
41/ 44 Minoo Desai
Marg
Colaba
Mumbai 400 005
Ph. 91 22 5638 5486

Abu Jani and Sandeep Khosla

Rs 5,000 onwards

The World is not Enough for this happening duo. Internationally acclaimed for their zardozi shawls and exquisite chikan kari, the designers' ethnic wear is lavishly strewn with resham, sequin and stone work; while their prêt line includes sanguine salwar kurtas, cape tops and indo-westerns. Exuding opulence, the showroom also displays their latest home furnishing collections. From Dimple Kapadia to Sophie Marceau 'The Boys' truly know how to bond with the best.

www.abusandeep.com
Mumbai@abusandeep.com

DAILY 10.30-6.30

'Loving Mother' Arvind
House,
9 Darabsha Road,
Off Napean Sea Road,
Mumbai 400 036
Ph. 91 22 2367 3401
MAP2 5

Adarsh Gill

Rs 10,000 onwards

Mrs G's, the toast of the French capital, creates magic with crystals and beads in her outfits, that shine even in cocktail parties back home. Plush white interiors set off unfussy silhouettes in abstract prints to make short kurtas and slim-fit trousers Cool pastels sprinkled with a joy of sequins on linens and

No 4, Sugra Manzil,
9 Best Marg,
Colaba, Mumbai 400039
Ph. 91 22 2284 1222/
2287 6063, **MAP2 6**

sheers adorn classic blouses teamed with straight-cut pants; while elegant saris with a related line of embroidered party bags go perfectly well with dripping diamonds and chic stilettos.

DAILY 10-7 (Sun closed)

Adidas

Rs 370- 7,000

Pump up your heart rate, Adidas is now neck-to-neck with big daddies, Nike and Reebok. High-tech trainers, tracks, boy-legs, jerseys, every kind of sportswear completed with accessories are making a spirited run through this shop. The small collection of striped and checked casual shirts in bold colours along with smart laptop bags, all spin the sporty look with a fashionable sprite.

DAILY 10.30-9.30

537 Linking Road, Opp. KBN, Khar (W),
Mumbai 400 052
Ph. 91 22 2649 0752/ 2646 5531

Unit 6, SkyZone, Phoenix Mill, Senapati Bapat Marg,
Mumbai 400 013
Ph. 91 22 2492 7868

Opp. Electric House,
York House,
1 & 2 Colaba Causeway,
Mumbai 400 039
Ph. 91 22 2282 2737

Shop 11, Atul Park
Sion-Trombay Road
Chembur,
Mumbai 400 071
Ph. 91 22 2556 3512

11, Hari Niwas
Lady Jamshedji Road
Shivaji Park
Mumbai 400 016

Aftershock

Prices on Request

With intricately beaded evening wear draped in flattering silhouettes and dreamy daytime dresses, Aftershock enters the Indian market with a graceful allure. Labels such as Rene Derhy and Little Buddha, along with an in-house range of hard-to-miss handbags and belts, add to the concoction here; so for a gilded look at guilty prices, beckon your shot of Aftershock for a pleasurable high.

kdon_55@yahoo.com
www.aftershockplc.com

DAILY 10-8.30

CR2 Shop No. 15
Nariman Point
Mumbai 400 021
Ph. 91 22 3951 9085

Aigner

Prices on Request

In 1904 Etienne Aigner was born in Hungary and a few decades later the world witnessed the birth of a brand selling great fashion accessories. Refined quality and subtly classy, the accessories available here include elegent silk scarves, leather wrist watches, well-crafted shoes and stylish handbags. The perfect destination to take your fiancé shopping, Aigner won't disappoint.

Grand Hyatt Plaza
Santacruz (E)
Mumbai 400 055
Ph. 91 22 5676 1234

Ajay Anand

Rs 500 onwards

Quaintly set, this store has furnishing material in cotton, raw and jute silk, jacquard and damask. Table linen and towels, along with a wide range of machine-made carpets, dhurries and unique coir floor coverings, add to the booty here. Pine-finished wood accessories include wine racks, trays and frames, all in a moderate-to-high price bracket.

DAILY 10.30-7.30 (Sun closed)

Rajul Apartments
Harkness Road
Malabar Hill
Mumbai 400 006
Ph. 91 22 2368 3985

Akbarally's

Rs 25 onwards

No surprises here, this departmental store has everything from casual Indian to formal western wear. Offering a wide gamut of products at fair prices and moderate quality, the store also stocks imitation jewellery, basic leather handbags, and cotton lingerie. Regardless of your budget, you can be assured of finding your day-to-day essentials at this large multi-purpose store.

DAILY 10.30-7.30 (Sun closed)

45 Veer Nariman Road
Mumbai 400 023
Ph. 91 22 2204 3921/4213

Sion Trombay Road
Chembur
Mumbai 400 071
Ph. 91 22 2522 0307/09

Aldo

Rs. 300 - 8,000

Specializing in high-quality products, this sought-after brand pays close attention to fine craftsmanship and cutting edge trends. Having its designers travel the world over to keep upbeat with new styles, Aldo makes sure that its customers remain at the pulse of fashion. Stylish and sophisticated, the products here are designed to please.

DAILY 10-10

Block No. 34,
Ground Floor
Phoenix Mills
462 Senapati Bapat Marg
Lower Parel
Mumbai 400 013
Ph. 91 22 2496 1634

Allen Solly

Rs 499 - 1,999

Established in 1744, this English brand has a range of semiformal clothing for men both, young and old. Although most popular for its 'indigo check' shirts, the brand also has t-shirts, jeans and trousers in monotone colours and basic designs. Tasteful and poised, the clothes here are ideal for business or pleasure.

FRI-WED 11-9.30 (Thurs closed)

14/ B S.V. Road, Santacruz (W), Mumbai 400 054
Ph. 91 22 2615 4786

Ram Murthy Road, Navpad, Thane 400 601
Ph. 91 22 2538 1601/ 2538 3610

201, Citi Centre
2nd Floor, S.V. Road
Goregaon (W)
Mumbai 400 062
Ph. 91 22 2878 9599

Shop No. 9, Sun Swift
Lokhandwala Complex
Andheri (W)
Mumbai 400 053
Ph. 91 22 2636 2560

Cousro Baug Shop, 8/A,
Opp. Bata Showroom
Colaba,
Mumbai 400 005
Ph. 91 22 2284 1554

Amarsons

Rs 100 - 1,00,000

Don't be intimidated by this conventional departmental store almost synonymous with shopping in Mumbai. An easily accessible shop, Amarsons provides an inexhaustible selection of goodies from baby bibs to Ravi Bajaj saris; with everything in multiple options and standard prices. So clutch on to your purses and elbow your way through, to find all that is coveted.

amarsons@vsnl.com
www.amarsons.com

TUE-SUN 11-9.30 (Linking Road)
DAILY 9.45-8.30 (Bhulabhai Desai Road)

296 Linking Road,
Bandra,
Mumbai 400 050
Ph. 91 22 26418880

63 Bhulabhai
Desai Road,
Mumbai 400 026
Ph. 91 22 2363
5551/53, **MAP2 7**

Amāyā

Rs 1,000 - 2,500

In an age where fashion extravaganzas head towards plunging necklines and rising hemlines, Amāyā offers conservative yet trendy clothing. The haute couture includes kurti tops contrasted with heavily embroidered bottoms, whereas the prêt line is fresher with stylized slit-sleeves, flowing crepe tops and linens trimmed with jute. The new 'Belly Blue' maternity line now offers comfort and style for the ballooning-belly days, with oh-so-cute dungarees, summery capris, and flowing dresses.

aditi_somani@hotmail.com

DAILY 9.45-6.30 (Sun closed)

Podar House, G. Floor,
'A' Road, Marine Drive,
Mumbai 400 020
Ph. 91 22 2284 5293
MAP2 8

Amber and Shirrin

Rs 1,800 - 42,000

While providing an excellent range of Indian and western clothing, Amber and Shirrin are most popular for their uniquely designed fusion wear. Elaborated with sequins, diamante and embroidery work, the Indian clothes give off a rich and stately look. The men's suits and women's business wear are also worth whisking through, while the shop's lovely scarves, beaded bags, and the breathtakingly beautiful jewellery steal the limelight.

www.aandsthestore.com
info@aandsthestore.com

DAILY 11-8.30

10, 'Quorum'
High Street, Phoenix
Senapati Bapat Marg
Lower Parel
Mumbai 400 013
Ph. 91 22 5661 0421

Amrapali Jewels

Rs 500 - 3,00,000

Welcome to the world of beauty and magnificence. Specializing in silver and gold ornaments, Amrapali offers an exquisite collection of ancient and ethnic jewellery.

62, Oberoi Shopping
Arcade
The Oberoi,
Nariman Point,
Mumbai 400 021

Dazzling semi-precious stones beautifully handcrafted in silver necklaces bring alive the memories of the maharaja epoch. Originally from Jaipur, this store is a popular destination with the crème de la crème of society, while its favourable location and attractive-show-window draws regular walk-ins and tourists.

amrapali@datainfosys.net

DAILY 10.30-7 (Sun closed)

Ph. 91 22 22843687 / 22024723

Ananya

Rs 1,500 - 50,000

Spot the trend as it happens in this chic boutique. From trendy indo-westerns and club wear by Aki Narula and Falguni & Shane to voguish accessories, Ananya translates couture to persona with its in-house brand and selective designer list. Leather jewellery with zircons say faux is in, while the shell embellished crochet bikinis make a serious fashion statement on the beach.

ananyabom@hotmail.com

DAILY 11-8 (Sun closed)

Shop No 3
Pluto Building
Turner Road, Bandra (W)
Mumbai 400 050
Ph. 91 22 26553327
MAP1 9

AND Designs/ Anita Dongre

Rs 400 - 2,500

If you are looking for prêt wear at affordable prices, AND Designs is definitely worth your time. Flowing shirts, cotton kurtis, and draw-string trousers in basic colours and practical cuts shadow the racks, while a small range of functional sportswear also finds its way here. In her traditional creations, Anita Dongre unveils salwar kameezes and lehengas, all which flourish in bright colour combinations and lavish embroidery detailing.

DAILY 10-8.30

Anita Dongre, Shop No 5,
Om Chambers, Kemps Corner
Mumbai 400 036
Ph. 91 22 2368 1946
www.anitadongre.com

AND Designs
Level 2, Crossroads
28 Pt. M.M. Malviya
Haji Ali Road
Mumbai 400 034
Ph. 91 22 2352 5138

Bajaj Niwas
Linking Road, Bandra
Mumbai 400 050
Ph. 91 22 2646 1886

Skyzone 4
Phoenix Mills
462, Senapati Bapat
Marg
Lower Parel
Mumbai 400 013
Ph. 91 98216 18123
andindia@vsnl.com

Anokhi

Rs 200 - 1,500

A part of the green scene, the clothes in Anokhi are made of vegetable-dyed fabrics. Using a salad counter concept, this indo-chic shop allows customers to mix-and-match cotton crushed skirts, sleeveless tops, and baby dresses, while the sarongs and handbags add a tasteful dressing. All those inspired by the hand-block prints, feel free to ask the servers, how all the ingredients are put together.

Rasik Niwas, Metro
Motors Lane,
Dr. AR Rangekar Marg,
Off Hughes Road,
Mumbai 400 007
Ph. 91 22 2368 5761
MAP2 10

www.anokhi.com
anokhi@anokhi.com

DAILY 10-7 (Sun closed)

Antè Body

Rs 7,000-1,20,000

Wooden interiors set off heavily worked garments in traditional blues, reds and greens. The predominant bridal wear saris and lehengas come from the likes of Nandita Thirani and Anju Modi, while a small selection of indo-westerns and salwar kameez make their way to the racks. The brainchild of Shalini Baheti, Antè Body takes you back in regal times and dresses you up to be queen.

Kwality House
1 Hughes Road
Kemps Corner
Mumbai 400 036
Ph. 91 22 23867115
MAP2 11

ante_body@yahoo.com

DAILY 10-8

Apparel Store

Rs 150 - 1,500

Lace up your sneakers, pull up your sleeves and dash into this dense fashion jungle. Expect to find yourself bombarded by export surplus garments, in-date with the latest international trends in every genre. Gym, casuals and maternity wear are also available here, while a dwindling collection of funky swimwear and accessories strive to be noticed. A value-for-money store for the ones who have time and perseverance at their disposal.

Surya Kiran Bldg
Paan Gali
Cumbala Hill Hospital Lane
Mumbai 400 036
Ph. 91 22 23804699
MAP2 12

DAILY 10.30-8

Araiya

Rs 250 - 14,500

If you are facing a fun evening out, with an uninspiring wardrobe, head to this double-decked store for a quick buy. Kurtas, lehengas, and saris occupy the lower floor, while faux leather pants, flowing shirts and dressy skirts funk up the upper level. To complete the chic look, suede belts dangle with tassels and imitation jewellery blush in their shy prices.

Shop No. 1
'Vasant'
3 A Peddar Road
Opp. Activity High School
Mumbai 400 026
Ph. 91 22 2351 0200

DAILY 10.30-8 (Sun closed)

Archana Kochhar

Rs 2,500 - 70,000

You might be daddy's little princess but if you still can't get him to shell out enough for a Tarun Tahiliani wedding outfit, welcome

20 Swastik Plaza
VM Road, Near Kala Niketan
JVPD Scheme

to your ivory tower. Heavily worked kurtis, saris and lehengas in rosy reds, frescoed with sparkling embroideries will b _ıten your special day; while bordering western garments in pearly pastels will frost your bridal closet.

archana@fashionhouseindia.com

DAILY 10.30-8.30 (Sun closed)

Vile Parle (W)
Mumbai 400 049
Ph. 91 22 26177 117/7253, **MAP1 13**

Arjun Khanna

Rs 40,000 onwards

Clean cut and judiciously embellished, the unpredictable silhouettes of this heralded designer are fervently cheered by his front-row couturiers. A dreamy mix of crisp fabrics and intricate details, the Mughal-inspired bridal and groom ensembles here, are fancily trimmed with silken threads. Unveiling a sharp sense for detailing and a keen eye on the palette, Arjun Khanna has his thumb firmly placed on the fashion pulse of the nation.

By Appointment Only

154C Ochiwada
Industrial Centre
Opp. Bus Depot
New Link Road
Goregaon
Mumbai 400 062
Ph. 91 22 2878 5923
MAP1 14

Arrow

Rs 595 onwards

Specializing in premium quality shirts for over a century, Arrow offers a complete range of men's wear from formals to sportswear. Tailored for the more permissive dress code of the present executive, the clothes are formal but easy going. Following international fashion trends, Arrow ensures a fashion-fit stitch in the corporate world.

acl.a20@arvind.sril.net

DAILY 10.30-8.30

Old Oriental Building,
MG Road, Fort,
Mumbai 400 023
Ph. 91 22 2267 0701, **MAP2 15**

19 Cusrow Baug,
SBS Marg,
Colaba,
Mumbai 400 001
Ph. 91 22 22882529/2283 2161

33 Malabar View,
Chowpatty
Mumbai 400 007
Ph. 91 22 2367 4341

2nd Rajdoot Apts,
Linking Road,
Khar (W)
Mumbai 400 052
Ph. 91 22 2605 0355

Ashish N Soni

Rs 2,500 - 15,000

Blacks, whites and greys are predominant in this sleek and understated designer boutique. This brother-sister duo signature line is distinctive for its extreme simplicity and precision cuts. With a restrictive use of embellishments to highlight form, the designers stress on fabrics and textures; the results translating into timeless and classic garments of the new millennium.

DAILY 11-8

Shop No.4,
The Courtyard
41/44 Minoo
Desai Marg
Colaba
Mumbai 400 005
Ph. 91 22 5638 5466/67

Atmosphere

Prices on Request

A plush showroom with beautiful drapes cascading down all corners, Atmosphere presents a truly international collection of silk and silk-blend fabrics. A venture of Himatsingka Seide Ltd, leading exporters of silk fabrics, this retail store sells luxury silks for furnishing, upholstery and drapes, all at glossy prices.

Vaswani House
BEST Marg
Colaba
Mumbai 400 039
Ph. 91 22 2283 1877

DAILY 11-7.30 (Sun closed)

Azeem Khan

Rs 15,000 onwards

Appropriately knighted as the 'crystal king' of fashion, Azeem Khan stands true to his name. From bridal saris to western outfits, the clothes are bold and vivacious with unconventional fabrics and daring colour combinations. Passionate about fuscia, Azeem Khan's forte lies in his fusion work, while his funky line of shoes match the theme of his outfits. Not for the light hearted or the light pursed, his creations will demand to be noticed by the gilt-edged of society.

Shop No. 1
Usha Sadan Building
Next to Colaba Post Office
Mumbai 400 005
Ph. 91 22 2215 1028/ 0372, **MAP2 16**

DAILY 10.30-7 (Sun closed)

Babubhai Bhavanji

Rs 35 - 12,500

Originally a supplier of fabrics, this store now offers ready-made clothing for men. Although most popular for its business wear, the shop also keeps a range of international branded shirts and t-shirts. Kurta pyjamas, sherwanis and windcheaters are available here as well; all at plain prices and of good quality.

Dadar T.T Circle
Mumbai 400 014
Ph. 91 22 2414 5459
MAP2 17

TUE-SUN 9.30-9

Bally

Prices on Request

Even better than cheese and chocolates – the scrumptious accessories from Bally come straight from the posh streets of Switzerland. Boasting of high quality and prices, the brand swings sophisticated handbags and wallets, along with well-styled footwear that walk like a charm. Also available is a 'natural bags' line. The entire range of products promise luxury and style. So, for a relaxed night out or a fancy cocktail party spell class with B-A-L-L-Y.

Grand Hyatt
Off Western Express Highway
Santacruz East
Mumbai 400 055
Ph. 022 56761234

www.bally.com

DAILY 8-10

Bambino

Rs 195 - 1,000

Where do you go to bundle up a bundle of joy? This garden-like store with flowery wall-paper, offers newborn girls up to the age of seven, the cutest of rompers, shorts, capri sets and floral dresses. Popular for its smocking thread work, this store adorns each of its products with frills, ribbons and bows; making every little girl wearing its outfits, the bonniest bambino in town.

DAILY 10-7 (Sun closed)

Sir Ratan Tata Institute
Annexe Ground Floor
30 N.S Patkar Marg
Mumbai 400 007
Ph. 91 22 2367 9161/62
MAP1 18

Bandhej

Rs 500 - 15,000

Combining a contemporary outlook with traditional textiles, Bandhej offers a range of prêt-a-porter salwar kameez, dupattas and a mix-and-match collection in cottons, knits and silks. Bandhej extends a great place for traditional shopping to the contemporary woman.

archana@bandhej.com
www.bandhej.com

DAILY 10.30-8

Grand Hyatt
Off Western Express Highway
Santa Cruz (E)
Mumbai 400 055
Ph. 91 22 3060 1011

F-26, Quorum 2
Phoenix Mill
462 Senapati Bapat Marg
Lower Parel
Mumbai 400 013
Ph. 91 22 2497 4050

Bar Code

Rs 240-1,540

A small shop carrying clothes for larger women, Bar Code stacks reasonably priced shirts, trousers and stoles. Made for classic dressing, the attires are simply designed with monotoned earthy colours and flowery prints; while the embroidered and cutwork pants lend flair to the entire range. If you are of bigger built and are looking for anything from casuals to business casuals, this shop is worth a stop.

barcodeclothing@rediffmail.com

DAILY 10.30-8

Store #7
Arsiwala Building
Wode House Road
Colaba,
Mumbai 400 005
Ph. 91 22 2215 3311/
2218 9083, **MAP2 19**

✹ Barbie

Rs 300 - 1,000

Glamorized as the perfect woman; every little girl has wanted to be like Barbie. Dreams can now be fulfilled in this new and official Barbie store, with clothes straight out of the diva's closet. Glossy and dainty, Barbie offers shorts and capris, flower-printed pants and glittery matching tops, in countless shades of peachy pinks, lime greens and lemon yellows. Designed for girls up to their pre-teens, the clothes are fun, effervescent and oh-so-frilly;

InOrbit Mall
Link Road
Malad (W)
Mumbai 400 064
Ph. 91 22 5643 0305

making us older women long for our childhood all over again.

barbiedesk@shirt-company.com

DAILY 11-8

Barefoot

Rs 200 - 3,000

Unearth your sensibilities with the textured flooring of this mystic store. The warm glow exhibits stylized cotton tunics and oomphy short dresses, perfect for mood indigo. Quirky handbags and interesting silver jewellery catapult the indo-chic look, while the footwear highlights are leather upturns by Edwin Pinto and denim flip-flops with snips of raw silk. Other titbits include one-off home and bar accessories. Tucked away in a garage, finding this alcove can be a treasure hunt, but hang on, the cache is sweet.

54 Meher Court
TPS4 Almeida Park
Bandra (W)
Mumbai 400 050
Ph. 91 22 26405629
MAP1 20

barefootnaturally@indiatimes.com

DAILY 11.30-8 (Sun closed)

Bata

Rs 54 - 5,000

Most Bata stores stock simple-looking rubber slippers, leather sandals and canvas tennis shoes. However, some of them like the flagship store have a variety of formal business shoes and tasteful party sandals. With cute kiddie sneakers in blues and pinks, the shop also offers brands such as Nike, Adidas and Reebok. Also available are leather bags, wallets and belts.

safi.bata@indiatimes.com

DAILY 10-9.30

Angria Estate Building, 3 Vincent Rd., Dadar
Mumbai 400 014, Ph. 91 22 2418 8010

Bismilla Building, Opp. Railway Station, Dadar
Mumbai 400 028, Ph. 91 22 2436 0453

808/ 2 Khusnum, Dadar T.T., Mumbai 400 014
Ph. 91 22 2413 7125

Gram Panchayat Rd., Goregaon (W), Mumbai 400 062
Ph. 91 22 2876 0291

Ness Baug Petit House, Nana Chowk, Mumbai 400 007
Ph. 91 22 2389 8691

388 Centenary Church Building, Grant Road
Mumbai 400 007, Ph. 91 22 2305 3301

Empire Building, 154 Dr. D.N. Road, Fort,
Mumbai 400 001, Ph. 91 22 2208 9713

Moosa Building, 433 Kalbadevi Road, Mumbai 400 002
Ph. 91 22 2201 6508

94 Linking Road, Khar (W), Mumbai 400 052
Ph. 91 22 269 3476

Bata Flagship Store
Nirmal Life Style Mall
L.B.S Marg
Ground Floor
Mulund (W)
Mumbai 400 082
Ph. 91 22 5555 4601/02

Samdhan Agarkar
Chowk
18 Sahar Road
Andheri (E)
Mumbai 400 069
Ph. 91 22 2834 2435

Sagar Avenue
Opp. Shoppers' Stop
Andheri (W)
Mumbai 400 058
Ph. 91 22 2670 6990

No. 5 Krishna Kutir,
Station Road, Andheri
Mumbai 400 058
Ph. 91 22 2623 6704

51 Hill Road, Bank of
India, Bandra,
Mumbai 400 050
Ph. 91 22 2645 6283

285/ 87 E.R.Road,
Bhendi Bazar,
Mumbai 400 003
Ph. 91 22 2340 9501

Shangrilla Shopping
Cent, L.T. Road,
Borivali (W),

Cosmos Commercial Centre, 3rd Road, Khar
Mumbai 400 052, Ph. 91 22 2648 6355

Daftari Road, Malad (E), Mumbai 400 064
Ph. 91 22 2881 3597

354 Matunga Mansion, Matunga,
Mumbai 400 019, Ph. 91 22 2418 0194

29 Ramratan Trivedi Road, Mulund (W),
Mumbai 400080, Ph. 91 22 2591 0747

Gordhandas Mansion, Opp. C.R.LY Workshop,
Lower Parel, Mumbai 400 012
Ph. 91 22 2410 4314

12 Station Road, Santacruz, Mumbai 400 054
Ph. 91 22 2605 6503

22 Swami Vivekanand RR. , Opp. Khira Nagar
Santacruz (W), Mumbai 400 054
Ph. 91 22 2614 7206

P 314 L J Road, Opp. Victoria Church,
Mahim, Mumbai 400 016, Ph. 91 22 2431 2023

2 Mohgebai Road, Vile Parle, Mumbai 400 057
Ph. 91 22 2613 1063

Ramodiya Mansion, 260, Dr. Annie Besant Road
Worli, Mumbai 400 025, Ph. 91 22 2437 4523

Saiudyan, Shop No. 6, Sector 14, Vashi
New Mumbai 400 073, Ph. 91 22 2789 8593

Sarvodaya Bhavan A-Wing,
Gokhale Road, Dadar (W)
Mumbai 400 028, Ph. 91 22 2432 5641

Elysium Mansion, Opp. Cusrow Baug, Causeway - Colaba
Mumbai 400 001, Ph. 91 22 2282 0379

Mumbai 400 091
Ph. 91 22 2861 7801

Oomrigarh Building,
115 Carnac Road,
Mumbai 400 003
Ph. 91 22 2342
955820/21

Sundar Apartments,
Chembur Circle,
Mumbai 400 017
Ph. 91 22 2529 1308

Plot No. 1A,
Chemburkar Marg,
Chembur
Mumbai 400 071
Ph. 91 22 2529 3856

35/37 K E M Hospital,
Avenue Road, Chika
Compound, Lower Parel
Mumbai 400 012
Ph. 91 22 2415 7774

Be:

Rs 600 - 5,000

Add froth to your wardrobe with vibrant creations from this eclectic store seething with affordable designer labels. Floral print skirts, silk halter tops and various shades of pants line the racks here, while embroidered and crushed shirts for men lounge in the background. Prying on a prêt Indian line, Be: also has hippy jewellery, kitschy bags and beachy chappals for the ultra-chilled look. As the store's slogan goes, 'be here or be there,' but wherever you are, we say, be noticed!

DAILY 10.30-8.30

Shop No. D, High Tide Building Plot No. 30/B Juhu Tara Road Santa Cruz (West) Mumbai 400 049
Ph. 91 22 26600280

F-6, Quorum, 1st Floor
Phoenix Mill, Block 2,
462 Senapati Bapat Marg
Lower Parel
Mumbai 400 013
Ph. 91 22 5661 2509

Kwality House,
Next to Cross Words
Below Kemps Corner Bridge,
Mumbai 400 036
Ph. 91 22 2382 5621

InOrbit Mall,
L-44, Ground Floor,
Mindspace, Link Road,
Malad (W),
Mumbai 400 064

Beauti Art

Rs 10 - 8,000

Those who are looking for the perfect bindi to complete their shringar should head straight to Beauti Art. Apart from the huge collection displayed at the shop, bindis can also be personalized and made-to-order here. Ethnic art jewellery, exclusive bangles and classic hair accessories complete the Indian look with a

Shop No. 7, R Mall,
L.B.S. Marg,
Mulund (W),
Mumbai 400 080
Ph. 91 22 2555 0825 / 0835

small hole in the pocket. So to complement your sparkle in every way, dot this name on your shopping list.

DAILY 10.30-10

Benu Sehgall Originals

Rs 1,400 - 1,00,000

Benu Sehgall recently opened her first retail outlet after 14 successful years of designing from home. Specializing in bridal and ethnic wear, she also has a prêt collection in indo-westerns and fusion attires. Extravagant embroidery, bright colours and quality fabrics are her passion while bandhanis and maangtikas are her style. Lavish and elaborate, say hello to the lady who believes in flamboyance full-throttle.

Quorum, 1st floor
High Street Phoenix
462 Senapati Bapat
Marg, Lower Parel
Mumbai 400 013
Ph. 91 22 5662 2075/6632

benusehgall@hotmail.com

DAILY 11-8

Benzer

Rs 50 onwards

A comprehensive family store, Benzer has something for everyone. Demarked in independent areas, the store offers everything from cute baby sets to ethnic wear for women and men, with variety galore. Look out for the imitation jewellery and cosmetic sections inside the store, while the rows of handbags at the entrance are hard to miss.

49 Bhulabhai Desai Rd.
Breach Candy
Mumbai 400 026
Ph. 91 22 2353 2266
MAP2 **21**

benzer@benzerworld.com
www.benzerworld.com

DAILY 11-8.30

Bhakti Creations

Rs 2,000-80,000

Specializing in Kutchhi bandhanis, this store is truly devoted to bandhej and designer gharchoras. An interesting palette of contrasting colours dye the silks, georgettes and crepes to make enthralling saris and lehengas. The fabrics are refreshingly devoid of embroidery or embellishment, which makes this shop an essential destination for some no-nonsense bandhani shopping.

89/91 Dhanji Mulji
Building, Ground Fl.
Old Hanuman Lane
Kalbadevi Road
Mumbai 400 002
Ph. 91 22 22057564

DAILY 10-8 (Sun closed)

Biba

Rs 500 onwards

Go Bollywood at this store that creates Indian and indo-western clothing for movie actresses and exhibits the same designs at its store. From salwar kameezes to kurtis teamed with parallel pants, Biba uses pure fabrics and embellishes them with floral prints and embroidery. With a tinge of filmy masala, this shop adds dhamaka to any bland wardrobe.

45- 54 Whitehall, Kemps Corner,
143 AK Marg,
Mumbai 400 036
Ph. 91 22 23675063
biba@bom5.vsnl.net.in

DAILY 11-9.30

F5 InOrbit Mall
New Link Road
Malad (W)
Mumbai 400 064
Ph. 91 22 2877 3565

CR2
Nariman Point
Mumbai 400 021
Ph. 91 98200 88959

Blackberrys

Rs 795 - 9,000

Mostly popular for its dress-line collection of suits and trousers, Blackberrys also has a range of casual clothing. Subtle coloured products in striped and plain designs mark the practical end, while a small range of cotton khakis, shorts and Indian wear fulfil casual wardrobe essentials.

The Mall Station Road, Malad (W), Mumbai 400 064
Ph. 91 22 2648 2970
retail@blackberrys.com
www.blackberrys.com

TUE-SUN 11-9

5 & 6
Khar Lotia Palace Co-op. Housing Society Ltd.
373 Linking Road,
Khar (W)
Mumbai 400 052
Ph. 91 22 2649 9999/ 2648 2970

Body Sport

Rs 100 - 5,000

Hop, skip and jump into this colourful sports store that stocks international brands in casual sports and fitness wear for everyone from the precocious 3-year-old to the grandfather trying to recapture his youth. High in quality and fair in price, the store specializes in sporty shoes, and gives its customers an overall fit shopping experience.

DAILY 11-9

3 Kapadia Chambers
Opp. Chhagan Mitha Petrol Pump
Dhobi Talao
Mumbai 400 020
Ph. 91 22 2201 4571

Bon Bon

Rs 345-1,495

There is nothing very bonny about it; it's just footwear in all its functionalities. The men's products include a basic selection of office shoes from Marco Ricci and Red Tape apart from the unbranded ones; while a wider women's selection has plainly designed platforms, block heels and boots. Also look out for the small children's footwear section, which borders on the cute bonbon zone.

DAILY 10-10

504 Linking Road
Khar
Mumbai 400 052
Ph. 91 22 26497 235

Versova Road
Andheri
Mumbai 400 053
Ph. 91 22 2634 0099

Boulevard Benzer/ Rocky S Jeans

Rs 1,200 - 80,000

Sport the va-va-voom street look and get dressed by the man who is responsible for Hrithik Roshan's and Bipasha Basu's style. Stylish jeans, zippy jackets and tattered tops make the prêt collection here ideal for the fashion-conscious youngsters; while glamorous lehengas and dazzling accessories leave divas and beaus gushing for more. For all those Townies who can't tread on to Boulevard Benzer, Rocky S Jeans provides some of the designer's best club and casual wear in a nutshell.

DAILY 11-8

Quorum, 1st floor
High Street Phoenix
462 Senapati Bapat
Marg, Lower Parel
Mumbai 400 013
Ph. 91 22 2497 3366/
0547, **MAP2 22**

Marine Apts, Juhu
Mumbai 400 049
Ph. 91 22 2618 1090

Boulevard Benzer
Santacruz Linking Road
Mumbai 400 054
Ph. 91 22 2646 2266

Brahma Selections

Rs 300 - 25,000

Every hue of the rainbow has a sari dedicated to it. Kanjivarams to Banarsis, gadhwals to dhakais and south cottons to organzas, the store brings us specialities from different regions of the country. Rolled in 30 years of tradition, Brahma Selections has now diversified into modern embroidery and fancy prints. Extremely busy throughout the day, it might be best to schedule your visit in the mornings.

DAILY 10.30-8 (Sun closed)

Chandralok 'A',
97 Napean Sea Road,
Mumbai 400 026
Ph. 91 22 2362 5610/
2363 7941

Bungalow Eight

Rs 1,500 onwards

This delightful shop chicly displays a plethora of home accessories and an occasional collection of stoles, sandals and other quirky fashion accessories. However the real eye-catchers are the serving bowls, salad servers and photo frames that are made out of which horn! Also on offer are delightful imports from the Far East, such as lacquered bowls and teak tables. Designed by Kapil Gupta, the store won the IIID award this year for Commercial Spaces. Warning-while driving here keep a keen eye on the road – this nook is easy to miss!

MON-FRI 10.30-7.30 & SAT 12-7

8 Carmichael Road
Mumbai 400 026
Ph. 91 22 2352 3427/
98206 04910, **MAP2 23**

Burlingtons of Bombay

Rs 1,000 onwards

Embroidered dinner jackets, sherwanis, office shirts, lehengas, saris, mojris...it's all here. A range of western and ethnic garments with flamboyant embroideries on

The Taj Mahal Hotel
Apollo Bunder
Mumbai 400 001
Ph. 91 22 2202 5593
MAP2 24

silks, linens and woollens, dress the whims of many a rich and famous world over, while the curios and accessories jam-pack the bags of visiting patrons. For the jet-setting clients, a 24-hour tailoring service is also offered here.

burlingtons@vsnl.net

DAILY 11.30-7.30 (Sun closed)

Calzarre

Rs 1,000 - 3,500

After producing shoes and accessories for European brands, Calzarre's debut in the Indian market has been a great success. Haute leather footwear and handbags are custom-made for the home masses in line with international quality standards. Strappy heels in lime-greens with coordinated bags for Sunday brunches, or closed maroon shoes for executive evenings make Calzarre the perfect destination while shopping for 'compliments'.

skexports@vsnl.com

DAILY 11-8 (Sun closed)

Quorum, 1st floor
High Street Phoenix
462 Senapati Bapat Marg
Lower Parel
Mumbai 400 013

10 - 11 CR2 Shopping Arcade, Nariman Point
Mumbai 400 013
Ph. 91 22 2497 0395

Cambridge

Rs 175 - 3,500

If you know the name, you probably know their business. Cambridge has been providing men's clothing for over 40 years. Striped, checked and plain shirts in basic colours are the brand's style, along with simple jeans and cotton pants. Sherwanis, jodhpuris and churidars form the Indian range, while comfortable kurta pyjamas are standard in design and price.

DAILY 10.30-8.30 (Sun closed)

Royal Collection
359 Dubash Building,
Shop No. 1, Ground Floor,
Maulana Saukat Ali Road,
Grant Road, Mumbai 400 007
Ph. 91 22 2386 6786/ 2384 0764

Shushil & Co.
44 A Bhawani Complex,
Bhawani Shankar Road
Dadar (W), Mumbai 400 028
Ph. 91 22 2437 3738/ 2437 9896

Supreme
No. 1, Kleen Co-op Housing Society
Opp. Railway Station, Santacruz (E),
Mumbai 400 055,
Ph. 91 22 2611 4634/ 2614 3498

British Cycle Co.
Kalbadevi, Mumbai 400 002
Ph. 91 22 2209 4650/ 2205 3545

Cambtex 4/5/6
A.N. House
31st Road
Opp. Bandra Talkies
Linking Road
Bandra (W)
Mumbai 400 050
Ph. 91 22 2645 2530/ 2645 4627

433 Kalbadevi Road
Princess Street
Opp. Madras Bhavan
Kalbadevi
Mumbai 400 002
Ph. 91 22 2209 4650
Mob. 91 98202 30948

Yess Boss
J.K. Sampat Marg
Near Plaza Cinema
Dadar (W)
Mumbai 400 028
Ph. 91 22 2434 9789/ 2432 9785

Cambridge Textorium
Kartan Bhawan
Colaba Causeway
Colaba
Mumbai 400 005
Ph. 91 22 2284 1410/ 2284 0250

2/B Kushrow Baug, Colaba Causeway, Colaba
Mumbai 400 005
Ph. 91 22 2284 1575

Canali

Rs 2,500 onwards

Muslin and puckered fabrics create unusual straight-bottomed shirts to be worn over yarn-dyed pants at this Italian brand. Flaunting plenty, from traditional classics to ethereal novelties, Canali has shoes in dark ochres and buttery soft buckskin belts. Its sportswear, includes a discreetly urban-minded collection, along with a carefree holiday range.

www.canali.it

DAILY 10-8

The Taj Mahal Hotel
Apollo Bunder
Mumbai 400 001
Ph. 91 22 2281 6828

Candy

Rs 695 - 2,000

This little shop has a variety of footwear for men and women. Offering a 'special' range of party shoes with bead and sequin work, Candy also has daily wear closed shoes, slip-ons and strappy sandals. Available in a range of colours and sizes, the shoes are refreshing and sweet–after all, that's what candy is made of!

DAILY 11-9

Shop No. 6
Khatau Mansion
Opp. Warden Road
Church
Mumbai 400 026
Ph. 91 22 2369 3160

Candy

Rs 195 - 10,000

Not to be confused with the entry above, this shop is a convenient place to replenish your depleting wardrobe. Casual and semi-formal salwar kameezes, kurtis and indo-westerns pay a tribute here. Sprinkled with sequins or strewn with threads, the store prides in embellishing each one of it garments with care and grace. On offer for the male counterpart is an entire floor dedicated to Tantra t-shirts and vegetable-dyed kurtis.

DAILY 10-8 (Sun closed)

49 Bhulabhai Desai Rd.,
Mumbai 400 026
Ph. 91 22 2351 1404/
23512148

Catwalk

Rs 450 - 4,450

As one of the better ped-poofers of the city, it is no wonder that Catwalk is a hot favourite with Miss India's and Gladrags' models. Featuring unique designs, the shop has chunky clogs, crystal heels and fashion trainers. Also serenading brides with sandals gussied up with zari work, and imported jute slippers, this shop

Piramyd Mega Stores
Cross Roads
Haji Ali
Mumbai 400 034

Kemps Corner
Mumbai 400 036
Ph. 91 22 2351 5890/
2351 5079

could easily raise any woman to feel like the cat's whiskers.

DAILY 10-10, DAILY 11-9 (Grand Hyatt Plaza)

Ground Floor Shop No. 9/10/11, MS Ali Road
Opp. Novelty Cinema, Grant Road, Mumbai 400 007
Ph. 91 22 2386 1494/ 2386 1495

Lokhandwala Complex, Andheri (W), Mumbai 400 058
Ph. 91 22 2636 2863

CR2, Nariman Point, Mumbai 400 021

InOrbit Mall
Ring Road, Malad
Mumbai 400 064
Ph. 91 22 2655 8888

Ramdas Naik Mark
43 Hill Road, Bandra(W)
Mumbai 400 050

Grand Hyatt Plaza
Santacruz (E)
Mumbai 400 055
Ph. 91 22 5676 1234

Caxton Sports

Rs 150 - 2,900

Fitness freaks, jump in. This store sports casual active wear and accessories, along with Indian cricket team shirts which can be personalized on request. Its counterpart, Action Sports is situated one store away and completes the gyming wardrobe, with a range of cycling shorts and fitted tops.

caxtonsports@vsnl.net

DAILY 11-8 (Sun closed)

4 & 4/A Kapadia
Chambers
Opp. Petrol Pump
Dhobi Talao
Mumbai 400 020
Ph. 91 22 2201 4299/
2205 2935

Central Cottage Industries

Rs 250 onwards

A typical tourist stop, this store is loaded with well-crafted souvenirs at high prices. Established during the 1950s in an attempt to sustain traditional handicrafts, the massive showroom is a reminiscent of the cottage industries of the country. Hand-painted wooden figurines, inlaid wooden items, teakwood elephants, carved stone gods, gold and silver jewellery and a wide range of carpets and dhurries make their way through here.

DAILY 11-7 (Sun closed)

34 Chhatrapati Shivaji
Maharaj Marg
Mumbai 400 039
Ph. 91 22 2202 6564/
22027537, **MAP2 25**

Chai

Rs 345 - 1,800

This designer store caters to all strata of society with its easygoing look and casual collection of clothing. Most popular for its denim dresses, Chai also serves party wear, knit tops and well-fitting suits. Its striped and woollen pants and military printed cargos are alluring, while its broad belts make a sweet side dish. For a chilled out evening or a relaxed afternoon tea party, you can definitely do with a serving of Chai.

chaiinfo@chaiwoman.com

MON-FRI 11-8
SAT-SUN 11-9

F19, Ist Floor
Quorum
High Street Phoenix
Lower Parel
Senapati Bapat marg
Mumbai 400 013
Ph. 91 22 5661 8514/
5661 8515

Charagh Din

Rs 330 - 5,000

25,000 shirts light up this one of a kind 4-layered shirt super store, which launches 15-20 new designs every day. The shop sells casual, business, golf and woollen shirts with a special range of churidar kurtas. Its 'Ditto' collection however, dittoes the spirit of the youth of Mumbai with a fling of zing and a toss of gloss; and those who can't access their way to the shop can now revert to the Internet to the store's online shopping basket.

charaghdin@charaghdin.com
www.charaghdin.com

DAILY 10-9

64 Wodehouse Road
Colaba
Mumbai 400 005
Ph. 91 22 2218 1375

Cheemo

Rs 495 - 6,000

Known for its versatility in design and consistency in quality, Cheemo keeps pace with global fashion trends. Its latest collection introduces silk handbags dazzling with crystals, and silver, perfect for ethnic evening wear; while a line of related embroidered chiffon scarves complete the imperial visage. Offering every colour of the rainbow, Cheemo is a definite destination for the perfect match to any outfit.

azeeexports@yahoo.co.uk
www.cheemoleather.com

DAILY 10.30-7.30 (Sun closed)

Mangal Darshan, Waterfield Road, Bandra (W)
Mumbai 400 050, Ph. 91 22 2643 2493

Shop 1, Natraj Apartments, Linking Road, Bandra (West)
Mumbai 400 050, Ph. 91 22 2640 5566

F60/61 H.C. Level
Oberoi Towers
Nariman Point
Mumbai 400 021
Ph. 91 22 2285 3497

44 Oberoi Towers
Nariman Point
Mumbai 400 021
Ph. 91 22 2285 3497

India House No. 2
Kemps Corner
Peddar Road
Mumbai 400 026
Ph. 91 22 2388 1558

Hotel Marine Plaza, 29,
Marine Drive
Mumbai 400 020
Ph. 91 22 2283 8347/
56371601, **MAP2 26**

Chemistry

Rs 400 onwards

A great destination for casual, sport and office wear, Chemistry offers an effervescent range of quality clothing at reasonable prices. Classic tees, cotton shirts and corduroy jackets in classic cuts are available here. Linen pants, patchworked jeans and track pants along with a range of mini skirts available here, promise chemistry for all you girls!

chemistry@estyleindia.com

DAILY 11-8

CR2
Nariman Point
Mumbai 400 001
Ph. 91 22 5654 7966

210, Govindham
TPS 3rd Waterfield Road
Bandra (W)
Mumbai 400 050
Ph. 91 22 2640 6601

Chic Baby

Rs 60-800

Nothing surprising yet nothing disappointing about this 22-year-old store, which stacks a

Marina Shop No. 1 & 2
Juhu, Mumbai 400 049

large range of casual western wear for newborns and children up to 14 years of age. Everything from night suits and bermudas to frocks and shoes can be found here, along with churidar-kurtas for boys and an indo-western collection for girls. The shirts with cartoon prints however, are especially cute and could make your little babies look ultra chic.

Ph. 91 22 2612 4007/ 2619 3228

DAILY 11-9

Choksi

Rs 25-400

All you charm queens, welcome to Mumbai's own answer to Accessorize. A huge selection of dangling earrings, pendants on ribbons and brass bracelets, puts this shop on the revered-list of young ladies 'rusting' for junk; while its colour-schemed organization, makes finding a quick-fix for a bland outfit as easy as possible. Other bits also include anklets, mobile chains and hair accessories.

18 Sunny Side, Opp. Domino's Pizza
Lokhandwala Complex
Andheri (W)
Mumbai 400 053
Ph. 91 22 2636 0259/ 2632 1407

DAILY 11-9

Chor Bazaar (Thieves' Market)

Rs 150 onwards

If you are conjuring up images of cloak-and-dagger intrigue and precious jewels with hushed histories, you're quite mistaken. Chor Bazaar is a fun place to rummage through an extravagant assortment of antiques, fakes, junk furniture and accessories. You'll find lampshades, rusty fans and dilapidated bric-a-bracs, all brimming with old-world charm. Hang on in all the mayhem here to find some real steals, but don't forget to bargain!

Mutton St.
Off Sardar Vallabhbhai Patel Rd
Mumbai 400 008

SAT-THURS 11am-7pm

Christina

Rs 50-7,000

Specializing in coordinates, the impeccably printed silks of this store have everything you might need for a completely matched ensemble. On offer are saris and poncho tops in a variety of designs, from traditional paisleys to abstract prints. Sizes vary from XS to XXXL. Leaving no desire unfulfilled, the shop also has cheery scarves and handbags that serve as elegant accomplices to the 'proper look'.

69, The Oberoi
Shopping Plaza
Nariman Point
Mumbai 400 021
Ph. 91 22 2282 5069

Valencia
Juhu Tara Road
Mumbai 400 049
Ph. 91 22 2660 6490/91

birdys@vsnl.com

DAILY 10.30-6.45

Citywalk

Rs 300 - 14,890

Situated in the heart of the frenzied Colaba Causeway, Citywalk offers every kind of shoe from casual and party to business and formal wear. Catering to all ages and needs, the shop offers a variety of slip-ons, sandals, and closed shoes in multiple colours and designs. Beaded bags with matching peds seem to be the shop's forte; sparing shopping women the hassle of haggling at other handbag stores.

DAILY 10-10

Kerawala Mansion
Carnac Road, Opp. Police Quarter, Mumbai 400 002
Ph. 91 22 2207 2977/2207 2968
info@citywalkindia.com; citywalk@vsnl.com
www.citywalkindia.com

33, Citywalk House
Colaba Causeway
Mumbai 400 001
Ph. 91 22 2285 6646/
22856647

Opp Khar Telephone
Exchange
Linking Road
Bandra (W)
Mumbai 400 052
Ph. 91 22 2600 5578 /
2600 6460, **MAP1 27**

Clothes Rack

Rs 250 - 1,800

The next best thing to shopping abroad; Clothes Rack has products from international brands like Banana Republic, Emporio Armani and Abercrombie & Fitch. Stacked in heaps, the clothes consist of casuals, gym gear and winter jackets. Offering true value for money with uncompromising quality standards, this shop is a somewhat unconventional shopping haven for those who are short on their budget and lavish in their time.

DAILY 10.30-8

Pooja Apartments, 17th Road, Next to Nalini & Yasmin
Khar (W), Mumbai 400 050
Ph. 91 22 2605 8800/ 2649 8902

264/ C- Amritlal Mansion, L.N. Road, Matunga (C.R.)
Mumbai 400 019; Ph. 91 22 2412 3394

93 Beach View
Shop No. 3
Opp. Tata Garden
Bhulabhai Desai Road
Mumbai 400 026
Ph. 91 22 2363 5059

Shop No. 73
Market Arcade
Cuffe Parade
Mumbai 400 005
Ph. 91 22 2218 7995

Safi Mansion
Irla - S.V. Road Junction
Vile Parle (W)
Mumbai 400 056
Ph. 91 22 2671 1396/
5695 0130, **MAP2 28**

Color Plus

Rs 1,000 - Rs 2,8000

This 100 per cent cotton international brand makes affordable casual and formal western wear for men. Sober coloured t-shirts, jeans, trousers, belts and wallets are predominant here, while its formal line, Purple Club, has stylish, jazzy shirts for all party animals. A small collection of women's shirts and tops are also offered here. A shop with high standards and a diverse variety of clothing, Color Plus is a good alternative to expensive designer wear.

sterling1@bol.net.in

DAILY 10.30-9 (Sun closed)

Shop No, 109
Heera Panna Shopping
Centre, Haji Ali
Mumbai 400 026

Colaba Causeway
Colaba
Mumbai 400 005
Ph. 91 22 2284 1821
191/192 Citi Centre
S.V. Road
Goregaon (W)
Mumbai 400 062
Ph. 91 22 2878 0179

Contemporary Arts & Crafts

Rs 150 onwards

An old favourite with Mumbai-ites, this treasure trove stocks household accessories from tableware and vases to candles and cutlery. On offer are handmade mother-of-pearl inlaid vases, ceramic aromatherapy burners, wooden furniture and rural handicrafts amongst other charming knick-knacks.

DAILY 10-8 & SUN 10-7

Opp BPL Mobile Showroom,
Napean Sea Road,
Mumbai 400 006
Ph. 91 22 2363 1979
MAP2 29

Cotton Lollypop

Rs 250 - 1,550

Lolled with casual wear, this shop has surplus clothes from various international brands. Shirts, t-shirts and bottoms can be found in their basic elements suitable for casual, sporty and easy wear; while an offbeat selection of 'shiny' shirts jazz up the shop's style quotient. Drop-in while scouting around the area, to find some cotton wears at lollypop prices here.

DAILY 10-9.30 (Thurs closed)

187 Citi Centre
SV Road
Goregaon (W)
Mumbai 400 062
Ph. 91 22 2878 3878

Cotton World Corp

Rs 200 - 930

The epitome of comfortable and casual clothing, CWC needs no further elaboration. This store provides high quality clothing ranging from t-shirts and shirts to shorts and pants, all in basic cottons of course. Simple and conservative, the products here are unmistakable in their soft look and caressing feel. But don't be surprised to spot your annoying neighbour wearing the same shirt as you; this shop has universal appeal.

DAILY 10-8

Ram - Nimi Building
Mandlik Road, Colaba
Mumbai 400 001
Ph. 91 22 5634 5555

Vipul Apartments
Tagore Road
Santacruz (W)
Mumbai 400 054
Ph. 91 22 2605 1602
MAP1 30

21/ 22 Nirmal Lifestyles
Mall, L.B.S. Marg
Mulund (W)
Mumbai 400 080

Cottons

Rs 495 - 895

What else would you expect from a store called Cottons? This 100 per cent cotton store has casual Indian and western clothing available in soft pastel colours for men and women. The saris are simple in their floral designs while the men's business and casual shirts provide comfort and quality, on a budget.

DAILY 9.30-9.30

Next to Kabutar Khana Market
Dadar, Mumbai 400 028
Ph. 91 22 2422 6268

Shop No. 4
Bileshwar Co-op
Housing Society Ltd.
Ganesh Gawde Road
Mulund (W)
Mumbai 400 080
Ph. 91 22 2564 3024/
2564 2813, MAP1 31

63/ 65, 1st Floor, World
Trade Centre
Cuffe Parade,
Mumbai 400 005
Ph. 91 22 22184495

Mangal Paridhan, Century Bazar, Century Bhavan
Dr. Anne Besant Road, Worli, Mumbai 400 025
Ph. 91 22 2438 5403

Next to Gazevo Restaurant, Bandra, Mumbai 400 050
Ph. 91 22 2646 5622

✹ Cottons (Jaipur)

Rs 195 - 1,500

This cotton warehouse has an affordable range of ethnic clothing and home furnishing, trucked in all the way from Jaipur. Traditional crinkled khadi-work skirts, printed kurtas and comfy kaftans deck up the racks here, while the exciting contrasts and the dramatic weaves have conferred on to the shop a heavy duty list of page-three customers.

3 Desai Mahal
19 Chowpatty Sea Face
Mumbai 400 006
Ph. 91 22 2368 5950

DAILY 10.30-7.30 (Sun closed)

Culture Shop

Rs 100 - 6,000

No culture shock here, this store is brimming with a mix of Indian-made ethnic and contemporary arts. Tantra t-shirts and printed kurtis align the racks while silk ties and trendy stoles swing effortlessly in their Indian aura. The selection in handbags includes traditional batwas, trendy purses and embellished jute bags, while the silver jewellery, handmade paper lampshades and brass accessories attract tourists galore.

Level 2 - Haiko Mall
Central Avenue
Hiranandani Gardens,
Powai
Mumbai 400 076
Ph. 91 22 5696 5800

info@cultureshopindia.com
www.cultureshopindia.com

DAILY 11-9

Curio Cottage

Rs 300 - 5,000

You no longer need to buy a new outfit for a party; just accessorize the old one differently. Offering a diverse variety of traditional and contemporary jewellery, this cottage has everything from delicate bracelets and long silver chains to ethnic armulets and chunky earrings. The beaded necklaces and stone studded pendants are truly outstanding, while the selection of belts and rings add a youthful tag to the shop.

19 Mahakavi Bhushan
Marg
Colaba
Near Regal Cinema
Mumbai 400 039
Ph. 91 22 2202 2607
MAP2 32

craftsindia@hotmail.com

DAILY 11-8 (Sun closed)

Cypress

Rs 700 - 4,000

With a cross section of designers such as Sabina Singh, Gavin Miguel, Umesh Jivnani, Gopi Vaid, Nilaya and Jaya Raheja amongst

Windward Apartments
21st Road, Khar (W),
Mumbai 400 052
Ph. 91 22 26461747
MAP1 33

others, welcome to Bandra's new fashion destination where the diverse range of clothes, jewellery, bags, footwear and watches, promise to dress every one from the bohemian babe to the indo-western woman. Whether it's a designer kaftan, a trendy poncho or an abstract two piece set you're looking out for, Cypress is not going to depress you.

DAILY 11.30-8.30

Dadar Emporium

Rs 150 - 25,000

In typical Mumbai fashion, this store towers over the many smaller sari stores in its vicinity. Simply interiored, the shop stacks a variety of saris ranging from Maharashtrian peshwais and Banarasi jamdanis to bridal zaris. So walk in, for a hassle-free buy at this unfussy and straightforward shop.

N.C. Kelkar Road
Dadar
Mumbai 400 028
Ph. 91 22 2422 1582

TUE-SUN 9-8.30

Daks

Rs 1,000 - 14,000

An interesting mesh of cream, camel, chocolate brown and charcoal, Daks' signature 'House Check' plays peek-a-boo with the finery and accompaniments available at this shop. Giving Burberry a run for its money, the collection at Daks is greatly inspired by the lifestyle and attitude of British aristocrats. A mix of patterns and detailing, the knits, jerseys, trousers and outerwear here, provide a smart collection for dashing dressers.

The Taj Mahal Hotel
Apollo Bunder
Mumbai 400 001
Ph. 91 22 5665 3366

DAILY 10-9 (Sun closed)

De Hauz Khas

Rs 3,000 - 45,000

Cheaper than a flight to Delhi and an attractive alternative to high-street designer shopping, De Hauz Khas platforms upcoming Delhi designers in Mumbai. Short salwar kurtas in georgettes and crepes, embroidered saris, and lehengas with heavily worked blouses, in a flurry of colours bedeck the racks. Prime in location and pleasant in ambience, the shop's charms have worked like magic on returning patrons.

Marine
Juhu Tara Road
Mumbai 400 049
Ph. 91 22 2660 8167

sherry@hauzkhas.com
www.hauzkhas.com

DAILY 11-7.30 (Sun closed)

Dee Jay

Rs 50 - 1,500

Between other run of the mill merchandise, Dee Jay's ethnic imitation jewellery stands out. Available in a variety of colours, the jewellery sets are made of white metal and are reasonably priced. Earrings, bangles with jhumkas and hair accessories available here are all worth fluffing through.

Shop 25, R-Mall
LSB Marg, Mulund (W)
Mumbai 400 080
Ph. 91 22 2591 4865

DAILY 11-9

Designer Studio

Rs 1,500 onwards

Strut your way into draping Indian luxuries and crystal butterflies. Haute couture from Rina Dhaka and Ravi Bajaj, and classic Kotwara chikan and zardozi art by Meera and Muzaffar Ali add to the sparkle and pizzazz here. Bold and glamorous, patrons get ready to be the stunner on that very special champagne-corking night.

Gr Floor, Vasundhara
Building
5 Bhulabhai Desai Road
Mumbai 400 026
Ph. 91 22 2351 6459
MAP2 34

designerstudio@hotmail.com

DAILY 10.30-7 (Sun closed)

Designs Unlimited

Rs 500 - 7,000

Funky denim jackets with innovatively placed zips, body-fit shirts and slinky halter tops find their place here. Specializing in men's club wear, the shop also has a small collection of suit sets and indo-western women's wear. Keen on providing highly personalized made-to-measure services, the shop's clothes are tailored to fit individual preferences and body-types.

G-29 Heera Panna
Shopping Centre
Haji Ali
Mumbai 400 026
Ph. 91 22 2351 0358

DAILY 11-9 (Sun closed)

Dockers

Rs 1,600 - 2,400

The khaki trend-setters, 'Dockers' from Levi's has redefined weekend wear. 100 per cent cotton t-shirts and checked smart-casual shirts in mixed and techno-fabrics are available here, along with semi-formals and office-wear trousers for the relaxed professional look. Although not a style platform, this brand has well-designed quality clothing, along with a selection of wallets, belts and caps to match. Dock here to deck up your weekend kit.

4/5 Shyam Vihar
Linking Road
Khar (W)
Mumbai 400 052
Ph. 91 22 2605 6388

DAILY 11-9

Ego

Rs 2,500 - 50,000

If you are facing a formal evening out, and can't find a handbag to match your designer outfit, this is the place to make your first stop. Distributors of international brands such as Fendi, Cartier and Lancel, Ego has products that speak of superb craftsmanship and distinct élan. With handbags offered in various sizes and designs, the store also sells bohemian wallets, belts and scarves to apprentice the classy act. In order to lighten your mood and also your purse, go ahead and pamper your ego.

The Courtyard
S.P. Centre
Store No. 12
41/ 44 Minoo Desai Marg
Colaba
Mumbai 400 005
Ph. 91 22 5638 5482

DAILY 11-8 & SUN 11-7.30

Empire

Rs 250 - 3,000

Adding to the plethora of shoe shops in Mumbai, this shoe territory is for all ages. More functional than stylish, you will find all the essentials with brands like Woodland, Red Tape, Lee Cooper and Nike. Shoes with sequins and crystals rein the women's section while the gents' and children's footwear is suitable for regular wear. More of a wander-in than a destination shop; Empire will fulfil your bare necessities.

Opp. Metro Shoes,
Near Shoppers' Stop
Andheri (W)
Mumbai 400 058
Ph. 91 22 2621 0231

Warden Road,
Mumbai 400 026
Ph. 91 22 2364 5455

Dadar TT, Dadar (E),
Mumbai 400 014
Ph. 91 22 2414 2164

DAILY 10-10

Enamour

Rs 500 onwards

Your grandfather went here, your father is going and soon, you will go too. Great quality clothing made one piece at a time, Enamour specializes in hand-embroidered sherwanis, kurtas and suits for men. Also stitching salwar kameezes for women and delightful scottish print dresses, and kurtas for children up to 10 years of age, this store enamours its customers with its vintage charm and simplicity.

Warden Road
Mumbai 400 026
Ph. 91 22 2354 0537

DAILY 10-7 (Sun closed)

Energy

Rs 450 - 1,050

Charge up your wardrobe with this no-nonsense store that has garments with sublime elegance for conservative women. More basic than bold, the store's casual clothing are spotted in sober colours with simple cuts. Crushed skirts, comfortable trousers and cotton kurtis line the shop's

Ram Nimi Building
8 Mandlik Road, Colaba
Mumbai 400 001
Ph. 91 22 2281 2870/ 2281 2867

hangers, while the small collection of men's trousers blend right in.

DAILY 9.30-10

Shop No. 9/A
Chinoy Mansion
162 Warden Road
Mumbai 400 026
Ph. 91 22 2364 2076

Ensemble

Prices on Request

The designer ensembles here are young and vivacious – spaghetti salwar kameezes, mermaid lehengas, and zardozi batwas – with names such as Tarun Tahiliani, Iksenya and Inky making their presence felt. Also flaunting classy clothing for the contemporary man, the clothes here are in vogue with the rich traditional look, promising you to sparkle and shine!

ensemblecrossroads@vsnl.net

DAILY 11-8

Great Western Building
130/ 132 Shahid Bhagat
Singh Road
Mumbai 400 023
Ph. 91 22 2284 3227/
2284 5167, **MAP2 35**

C - 223
226 - 228, Crossroads
28 Pt. M.M. Malviya Rd
Haji Ali
Mumbai 400 034
Ph. 91 22 2352 5164/
2352 2064

✷ Ermenegildo Zegna

Rs 3,000 onwards

Luxury men's wear doesn't get more luxurious than this. Muted interiors offset precision tailored clothes while an eye for detail and quality extends to the sales staff trained in Milan. A world-class collection of formals personify structured elegance, while the casuals and sportswear collection is made using latest fabric technologies for weekending in style. The treat extends to a fine selection of materials for the made-to-measure service; and presto, your suit is flown out straight from Italy for the final fitting.

www.zegnaermenegildo.com

DAILY 10.30-8

28, Crossroads,
28 Pt. M.M Malviya Rd.
Haji Ali,
Mumbai 400 034
Ph. 91 22 5660 3085/
56603086

Estelle

Rs 50 - 3,500

This 15-year-old Indo-Canadian venture has proved its metal to young satisfied customers with its elegant products. Gold and silver-plated, the jewellery ranges from chains, and pendants to bracelets and earrings. Subtle and durable, the wide variety of sets, crystal-studded bracelets and antique-finished neck pieces are especially popular here; all that promise to make your delicate wrists clang in approval.

celcorp@vsnl.com

DAILY 10.30-10

Shop # 33, Fun Republic
Opp. Laxmi Indl. Estate
New Link Road
Andheri (W)
Mumbai 400 053
Ph. 91 22 5699 4831/
5699 4832, **MAP1 36**

13 Tirupati Apartments
Bhulabhai Desai Road
Opp. Mahalaxmi Mandir
Mumbai 400 026
Ph. 91 22 2492 7481/
2492 2330

Eternia

Rs 50 onwards

Eternia the ladies department at the Premsons Bazaar, caters to all ages. For a complete make-over of a feminine wardrobe, everything from casual t-shirts and pants to formal salwar kameezes and crushed skirts can be found here. Offering a collection of heavily-beaded purses and large varieties of imitation jewellery including its very popular evil eye products; this nicely groomed store is a refreshing respite amidst the otherwise hectic bazaar.

Level 1
Premsons House
Breach Candy
Mumbai 400 026
Ph. 91 22 2363 6600
MAP2 37

gala@giasbm01.vsnl.net.in

DAILY 9-9 (Sun closed)

Fabindia

Rs 190 - 2,000

The craftsmen of 'gram-udyogs' from rural India cater impartially to all sizes and pockets at this store. You will find everything from saris and shirts to juties in silk and cotton handlooms, worked with regional specialities such as ikkat work, kalamkari and baagh prints. Nehru jackets, crushed skirts and angrakha tops in earthy colours make an artsy style statement, while the equally popular home furnishing section is worth surfing through.

137 M.G. Road,
Kalaghoda,
Mumbai 400 001
Ph. 91 22 2262 6539/
2262 6540

No 2 & 4, Navroze,
Near HDFC Bank,
Pali Hill, Bandra (W),
Mumbai 400 050
Ph. 91 22 2646 5286/
2646 5289, **MAP1 38**

F Wing 2, First Floor
InOrbit Mall Mindspace,
Link Road
Malad (W)
Mumbai 400 064
Ph. 91 22 5641 9989

Jeroo.bombay@fabindia.com
www.fabinidia.com

DAILY 10-7.45 (Mon closed)

Faith

Rs 390 - 1,800

After roaming all the shoe stores of Mumbai and almost losing faith, this shop may offer something different. With shoes imported from abroad along with in-house designing, this shop carries a diverse range of footwear from ethnic kolhapuris to catty suede boots. The men's collection of leather shoes looks especially promising, while the women's wedding sandals stand tall in their elegance and poise.

Chinoy Mansion
Warden Road
Mumbai 400 036
Ph. 91 22 2367 3991

F - 40
Oberoi Towers
Mumbai 400 021
Ph. 91 22 2285 6006

DAILY 11-9

Fendy Shoes

Rs 495 - 3,000

If the superfluity of leather and shoe shops in the Oberoi Shopping Arcade hasn't depleted your will to shop, Fendy is worth a visit for its reasonable selection of ladies sandals. A keen

F-83 Oberoi Shopping
Arcade
Nariman Point
Mumbai 400 021
Ph. 91 22 2281 5571

eye on the racks will discover a few niche designs apart from the common ones available elsewhere. Not a planned stop but more of a stroll-in, Fendy requires your time to spare and will to surf.

DAILY 11-7.30 (Sun closed)

Fila and Proline

Rs 100 - 7,500

Revamp your gym gear with products from this store that offers sports clothes and accessories from two international brands. Found here are dual purpose dry-fit shorts, used for both, workouts and swimming, while their one-of-a-kind, pique polos play the classic act. Additionally, the shop also offers casual tees, sports jackets, shoes and a small range of Ferrari products.

1-6/706, Shyam Vihar
Linking Road, Khar (W)
Mumbai 400 052
Ph. 91 22 2649 5833/
2648 3246

sunders@batragroup.com

DAILY 10.30-9.30 (Sun closed)

Sunders, 1 Yusuf Building, Flora Fountain
Mumbai 400 023, Ph. 91 22 2648 3246

Finlay's

Rs 400 - 2,500

When Finlay's says it is cotton, it is pure cotton. A nearly 100-year-old textile major has made a recent entry in the ready-made garment segment; making quality along with price its USP. 95 grams cotton shirts, kurta pyjamas, saris, salwars and children's clothings are made in organdie, cambric, lawn and terry-rubia here. A Govt. of India undertaking, this brand aims at providing affordable clothing to its age-old patrons.

Marina Mansion
SVP Road
Chowpatty
Mumbai 400 007
Ph. 91 22 2362 0595
MAP2 39

MON-SAT 10-9, SUN 1-9

Floral

Rs 50 - 9,000

Girls will be girls and boys will be boys – this is why Floral is divided into two sections of casual daily wear clothing and accessories for newborns to children 15 years of age. Everything in casual and nightwear can be found here, along with a wide range of shoes to match. Don't forget to peep into their 'special room' either, which has miniature suits for boys and tiny salwar kameezes for girls.

Devchhaya
Ground Floor
Tardeo Road
Haji Ali Corner
Opp. Crossroads
Mumbai 400 034
Ph. 91 22 2494 1100/01

floral.in@vsnl.net

DAILY 9.30-9

Footsie

Rs 395 - 1,095

Embarrassed of playing footsie with your significant other because of your tattered old shoes? It's time to hit the shops and get your pretty feet some new attire. Footsie offers a wide collection of casual and formal shoes for men and women, while its true speciality lies in its Indian range of colourful mojris. Small but well-stacked, this shop aspires to cater to your every desire.

164 Chinoy Mansion
Kemp's Corner
Mumbai 400 026
Ph. 91 22 2364 1253

DAILY 11-8.30 (Sun closed)

Frazer and Haws

Rs 350 onwards

Established in 1869, this silver house presents us with exclusive designs, which are both classy and contemporary. A wide range of sterling sliver collectibles and jewellery are on offer here. Sophisticated interiors create an opulent ambience befitting the image of its parent company, Hennell from London, and houses brands Homer and Scarpia as well. The Indian boutiques pay homage to the regional religious and cultural aesthetics in their designs.

3 Landmark Building
Pali Naka
Off Turner Road
Bandra (W)
Mumbai 400 050
Ph. 91 22 5675 0880
MAP1 40

frazer@frazerandhaws.com
www.frazerandhaws.com

DAILY 10.30-7 (Sun closed)

Freelook

Rs 329 - 749

One to 14-year-olds, step in, and look freely at the products in this store. Made of cotton and linen, the casual clothing, consist of shirts, spaghettis, skirts, and trousers, all in refreshing colours and cute designs. Fashionable and totally 'with-it,' the attires are especially sprinkled with fluttery butterflies for giggly girls and smart stripes for He-Man boys.

Shop No. 14
Heera Panna Shopping Centre, Haji Ali
Mumabi 400 026
Ph. 91 22 2351 4787

U - 31, InOrbit Mall
Mindspace, Link Road
Malad (W)
Mumbai 400 064
Ph. 91 22 5643 0433

DAILY 10.30-9.30 (Sun closed)

Frenzy

Rs 450 - 2,000

Are you in a frenzy to buy some functional, daily wear shoes? This shop might just be able to fulfil your needs. Made with moulded Italian soles, the strappy sandals and wide heels are light and comfortable. Formal leather shoes in the men's range boast in variety here, while the

158 Chinoy Mansion
Warden Road
Mumbai 400 036
Ph. 91 22 2368 1781

feminine collection of mojris are pretty and prominent.

DAILY 11-9 (Sun closed)

Fuel

Rs 1,000 - 9,000

Housing creations of top-notch designers like Suneet Varma and Raghuvendra Rathore, Fuel dresses to impress. Prismatically coloured westerns are the mantra of the shop, while the sophisticated kurtas match up in pomp and aplomb. The funky bags and shoes serve to fuel your already hot and flaming wardrobe, while the jewellery promises to emblaze your ensemble with a touch of silver.

Kantilal Karia & Co.
Chowpatty View Bldg.
Opp. Sukh Sagar
Mumbai 400 007
Ph. 91 22 2369 3131/ 2369 7171, MAP2 41

fuelindia@rediffmail.com

DAILY 11-8

✹ Fun Clothing Co. Pvt. Ltd.

Rs 200 - 600

Clothes so cute you wish you could fit into them. Earthlings' and Sugarplum's tiny cargos, Hawaiian tops and darling dresses for infants and girls will make your heart melt. While the windbreaker jackets and surf tanks bring about boyish glees, the 100 per cent pre-shrunk cottons in athletic and beach wear are delightful and comfortable; with prices to match. FCC has it all for your junior hipsters and babies-around-town, to truly look like sugar and spice and everything nice.

No. 8, 'A' Wing, Royal Classic,
Next to Fame Adlabs & Citi Mall,
New Link Road,
Andheri (W),
Mumbai 400 053
Ph. 91 22 2630 3437
MAP1 42

mail@funcco.com

DAILY 11-9.30

FuToes

Rs 695 - 2,000

The problem with good-looking shoes is that most of them leave your feet sore. This shop however claims to have fashionable footwear accompanied with comfortable fits. Specializing in daintily embellished shoes, the store also platforms sassy sandals and chunky leather boots; while men can keep busy with a more modest collection of basic shoes offered here.

Shop No. 1 & 2
Khatau Mansion
Opp. Warden Road Church
Mumbai 400 026
Ph. 91 22 2367 5169
MAP2 43

Oberoi Shopping Centre
2nd Floor
Nariman Point
Mumbai 400 021

DAILY 11-9

Lokhandwala Complex, Lokhandwala
Mumbai 400 058

Gabbana

Rs 750 - 85,000

A fashion destination for the prêt, haute, sport or street look, Gabbana lauds its international brands of Just Cavalli, DKNY, and D&G. The expansive collections range from Indian and western clothing to handbags, ties and shoes, all presented to you by the illustrious Akbar Shahpurwala. Although the 'Green Room' is used for personal appointments with long standing and VVIP clientele, all customers are promised superior quality products and service.

DAILY 10.30-8.30

4, Tirupati Arcade
Bhulabhai Desai Road
Opp. Mahalaxmi Temple
Mumbai 400 026
Ph. 91 22 2493 0692/3
MAP2 44

Junction of 15th Road
Next to Thribhuwandas
Bhimji Zaveri, Khar (W)
Mumbai 400 052
Ph. 91 22 26480
100/ 200

✱ Galleria

Rs 550 - 4,000

A hot-stop shop with tinsel town biggies, Galleria has an electrifying collection of clothes and accessories for youngsters. This finger-on-the-pulse store brings the hip disco-style of the West to the country. Prices are on the moderately higher-end, but so is the style, with glittery appliqué tanks and slash tees. On the frills spectrum, the products range from the latest plastic sandals to ruche boots and cool beach bags to cute hats. Galleria truly has all you need to be crowned a 'fashion diva'.

shamildavar@yahoo.co.in

DAILY 10.45-8.45 (Sun closed)

Near Ananya, Turner Road, Bandra (W),
Mumbai 400 050, MAP1 45

4 Juhu Princess
Juhu Tara Road
Mumbai 400 049
Ph. 91 22 5699 9314

10 Foreshore Apts
Opp. Kimaya
Juhu Tara Road
Mumbai 400 049
Ph. 91 22 2614 3229

Shop No. 8
Samarth Vaibhav
Comm. Complex
Lokhandwala Complex
Off New Link Road
Andheri (W)
Mumbai 400 053
Ph. 91 22 5698 7247

Garden

Rs 243 - 4,000

An established name in India, Garden specializes in flower-printed saris and salwar kameezes on pastel monotones, that bring out the feminine side of a woman. Chiffons, crepes and polyesters are particularly popular here, while the polka-dotted and striped prints add a joyous frolic to the Garden. The festive seasons also bring with them heavily beaded and embroidered saris to join the celebration.

DAILY 10.30-7.30

Garden Studio Line
Cecil Court, Near Regal Cinema
Colaba Causeway, Colaba
Mumbai 400 039
Ph. 91 22 2202 7825

'Smruti' Bhulabhai Desai Road
Opp. Tirupati Apartments
Mumbai 400 026
Ph. 91 22 2352 2268

Fresh Up 806, Empire Mahal, Dadar T.T.
Mumbai 400 028
Ph. 91 22 2412 0750

Gini & Jony

Rs 245 - 1,665

Hurray! Children from six months upto 16 years of age can find a bright supply of clothing here. With a mix and match approach, Gini & Jony makes expanding a child's wardrobe easy, especially with such reasonable prices. Spaghettis, hats and socks add a dose of fun to the girls' closets, while the boys can look cute in the sunglasses, jeans, and sports shoes available here.

mahalaxmi@lp.giniandjony.com

DAILY 10-9

Madav Kunj Apartment
A Wing, Shop No. 1 & 2, Borivali, Mumbai 400 091
Ph. 91 22 2861 2087

Arihant Industrial Estate, 118 Kranti Nagar
Sahi Veehar Road, Opp. Shetty Chemicals, Andheri (E)
Mumbai 400 072
Ph. 91 22 2847 2692/ 2847 2693

705 Sham Kunj, Linking Road, Next to Nike Showroom,
Khar (W), Mumbai 400 052
Ph. 91 22 2649 7556/2604 7482

Shop No. 11
Mahalaxmi Tirupati
Shopping Arcade
Opp. Crossword
Bhulabhai Desai Rd.
Mumbai 400 026
Ph. 91 22 2492 6696
MAP2 46

130/ 132 Great Western Building
Shahid Bagat Singh Road
Fort, Mumbai 400 023
Ph. 91 22 2287 2882/ 2284 3227

A/2 474 Shah & Nahar, Industrial Estate
Lower Parel Compound,
Mumbai 400 013
Ph. 91 22 2494 2126/ 2498 3136

Globus

Rs 50 onwards

No surprises here; this large and comprehensive departmental store has something for everyone. From baby bibs to heady hats and slinky slacks to beaded bracelets, this shop provides it all. With products from all over the globe, Globus takes its customers for a fashion joy ride, and asks for level-headed fares in return.

DAILY 10.30-9.30

Hill Road, Bandra (W)
Mumbai 400 050
Ph. 91 22 2643 6070
MAP1 47

Gold Leaf

Rs 1,500 onwards

There is nothing out-of-the-blue at the Gold Leaf. A regular parade of indo-westerns and Indian ethnic wear embellished with zardozi and crystal works make their appearances here; while semi-formal kaftan-tops in synthetic mixes look comfortable in their place. Customized bridal lehengas and made-to-order outfits can be arranged with in-house designers as well.

gold_leaf@bom5.vsnl.net.in

DAILY 10.30-7.30 (Sun closed)

Shop No 9, Natraj Building, 68 Hill Road, Bandra (W),
Mumbai 400 050. Ph. 91 22 2640 0897

Shop No 4, Sea Palace,
254 Juhu Tara Road,
Mumbai 400 049
Ph. 91 22 2660 9371

Golden Thimble

Rs 5,500 onwards

This cottage-like shop with oak panels and wooden furniture offers elegant Indian and western clothing for women. Come prepared to be swept away in the land of ivory and pearl-studded blouses, lehenga saris, and halter tops with beaded pants. As one of the few designer stores to have wearable clothing at affordable prices, Golden Thimble is an inviting stop on any trousseau shopping extravaganza.

18/20, K. Dubash Marg
Kala Ghoda, Fort
Mumbai 400 023
Ph. 91 22 2284 2598/ 2284 4206, **MAP2 48**

gtshaina@yahoo.com

DAILY 11-7 (Sun closed)

Usha Kunj, Jn. of Juhu Tara Road,
Santacruz (W), Mumbai 400 054
Ph. 91 22 3803 3884

Golden Touch

Rs 800 - 3,000

The flagship store of 'Soled Out' and 'Gossip', Golden Touch stocks a colourful selection of beaded, crystal and leather sandals, that regularly feature in fashion magazines. Vouching for its superior quality, the store also lends a Midas touch to any outfit by offering shoes that are made to wow.

F/35 H.C. Level Oberoi Towers
Nariman Point
Mumbai 400 021
Ph. 91 22 2204 2336

golden_touch@hotmail.com

DAILY 10.30-7 (Sun closed)

✷ Good Earth

Rs 150 onwards

Glass votives in jewel tones, candelabras in antique brass and marble bowls with shell inlay add a special touch to the home décor accessories here; while the bamboo water-pieces, incense sticks and bath indulgences are perfect to recreate a Balinese spa in your house. Furniture made of banana leaves and other materials are decorated amidst studio pottery and silk cushions on the store's upper level. A good choice for buying a gift or accessorizing your own space, Good Earth is full of paraphernalia that can make your heavy purse light.

Raghuvanshi Mills
Lower Parel
Mumbai 400 013
Ph. 91 22 5572 0345/ 5572 0342, **MAP2 49**

www.goodearthindia.com

DAILY 10.30-7.30

3 Cornelian, 104 August Kranti Marg
Kemps Corner, Mumbai 400 036
Ph. 91 22 2389 1084

Green Bell

Rs 50 onwards

A lush store carrying clothing for tads up to the ages of five, this shop is evergreen with miniature fashion products. From baby suits and swimming costumes to thermal wear and bath robes, this cushy zone also reveals international brands like Guess and Next Kids. Maternity clothing for all you mommies in-the-making is all available here; so make sure you go ring this bell.

DAILY 10-10

Vaishali Shopping Centre
Next to Baby Bell
V.M. Mehta Road
Juhu Scheme
Vile Parle (W)
Mumbai 400 049
Ph. 91 22 2611 7157/
2618 5416, **MAP1 50**

Green World

Rs 120 - 10,000

Hard to miss, this large departmental store has products for every member of the family starting from chubby-cheeked babies to silver-haired granddaddies. Stacked up in chalk-a-block piles, the clothes are enthusiastically showed off by ambidextrous salesmen. Brands such as Zodiac, Pepe and Color Plus are also witnessed here, while a collection of shoes, undergarments and sports gear add to the foliage.

DAILY 10-10

Sagar Garden
L.B.S Marg
Mulund (W)
Mumbai 400 080
Ph. 91 22 5599 3991/92

H. Couture

Rs 900 - 7,500

Shirts made of natural fibres and earthy colours line the racks of this store, which has Indian, indo-western and western wear for men and a small range of indo-western shirts for women. Catering to the conservative yet trendy, the store has clothes with simple pin-tuck designs and fine cuts. Well designed with a classy cottage-like ambience, this alcove delivers loungy clothes for champagne brunches and indigo moods.

hcouture2000@yahoo.co.in

DAILY 10-7.30 (Sun closed)

Motilal Mansion
17 Napean Sea Road
Mumbai 400 036
Ph. 91 22 2368 4710
MAP2 51

Habit Shoes

Rs 395 - 3,000

Redone a year ago, this squeaky clean shop claims to have shoe designs that are not available anywhere else in the market. Specializing in beaded work, the shop offers shoes in leather, suede, and synthetic materials. Flaps, clogs, and mojris for every age are available here and can be bought at fair

Shop No. 6
Metro House Causeway
Colaba
Mumbai 400 005
Ph. 91 22 2281 4555

Kemps Corner
Mumbai 400 036
Ph. 91 22 2363 1044

prices – after a good amount of bargaining of course!

DAILY 11-9

Hakoba

Rs 800 - 16,000

Especially known for its embroidery work, this white-interior store blossoms with pastel flowery designs on salwar kameezes and saris. Its bright crushed dupattas lend a youthful spirit to the shop, while men can get Indian outfits custom made here to add understated elegance to their wardrobes.

mumbai@pelhakoba.com

DAILY 10.30-8.30

Fancy Embroidery, Lokhandwala Complex
Opp. Bank of Maharashtra
Andheri (W), Mumbai 400 058
Ph. 91 22 2631 1442

Sector 17, Near McDonalds, Vashi, Mumbai 400 703
Ph. 91 22 2789 3784

Shop No. 1 & 2
Tirupati Apartments
Breach Candy
Mumbai 400 006
Ph. 91 22 2492 7888

Shop No. 15
Cusrow Baug
Electric House, Colaba
Mumbai 400 005
Mob. 91 98200 48660

Hangten

Rs 299 - 1,200

Hang in there for a ten-on-ten American fashion experience. This US brand offers its country's daily-wear clothing to dudes, dames and broods. Comfortable shorts, pants, and jerseys along with a selection of sportswear can be found here. So if you have recently been bitten by the American bug, quit feigning that accent and head over to this 'cool' store.

hangtenp@hotmail.com
www.hangten.com

DAILY 10.30-9.30

Shop No. 5, Skyzone
Phoenix Mills
462 Senapati Bapat Marg
Lower Parel (W)
Mumbai 400 013
Ph. 91 22 5660 2932

Centre 1 Shopping Mall
1st Floor, Vashi
Mumbai 400 703
Ph. 91 22 2781 2128

Hast Kala

Rs 400 - 50,000

Literally meaning 'Hand Skill', this shop has etched a name for itself in every Mumbai household. Providing its customers with a range of saris, from different parts of the country, the shop's main forte lies in its designer drapes from Kolkata. Materials used are mainly pure cottons, crepes and georgettes, while a few synthetic mixes also find their way in.

hastkalasarees@vsnl.com
www.hastkalaonline.com

DAILY 10-9 (Sun closed)

3 Tirupati Apts
Bhulabhai Desai Road
Mumbai 400 026
Ph. 91 22 2491 9901/02/03, MAP2 52

Hidesign

Rs 500 onwards

This shop is about skin that looks better with age. From bags to belts, jackets to wallets, the shop offers genuine leather goods in contemporary design. Stringent quality control measures at every process from tanning to stitching, make this brand a reliable investment for those yearning for age-free products.

DAILY 10-8 (Sun closed)

India House, Kemps Corner
Mumbai 400 036
Ph. 91 22 23869188

Oberoi Shopping Arcade
Nariman Point
Mumbai 400 021
Ph. 91 22 22845317

30B Juhu Tara Road
Mumbai 400 049
Ph. 91 22 26610560
MAP1 53

High

Rs 50 - 3,000

Clothes here spunk up your wardrobes, with all the junk and funk you need to get punked. A kitsch selection of ripped denim skirts, and skimpy halters stack the female racks; while the gunjee shirts, jackets and ghetto-style pants for men add to the coolness. Spiked handbags and other groovy accessories prickle the senses; all racing you up, biker-style high.

DAILY 11.30-9.30, SUN 2.30-9.30

142 Waterfield Road,
Bandra (W),
Mumbai 400 050
Ph. 91 22 5678 7464

High Street

Rs 750 - 70,000

This small shop has been steadily climbing the charts for good quality wear for men. Although popular for its sherwanis and suits, the store also has formal shirts with Indian prints, chikan kari churidars and embroidered mojris. For the groom's wedding attire, or even for one of his side functions, nudge this store high up on the shopping list.

director@highstreetbombay.com
www.highstreetbombay.com

DAILY 10-9

512 Linking Road
Bandra (W)
Mumbai 400 050
Ph. 91 22 2649 8909

Himation

Prices on Request

A frosty-pink showroom with a stroke of gold, Himation presents a natty collection of sassy clothes and accessories. Purring out to the elite; the effervescent and swish cache here looks straight out of the latest *Vogue*. Sexy short dresses and cigarette pants to chic pointed sandals and chromatic arm-slip purses, the international brands available here are all set to make you the cynosure of every eye (read guy). Glide in girls, to slip into a Prada or Gucci.

DAILY 11-8.30, SUN 3-8

Below Cumbala Hill
Bridge,
Kemps Corner,
Mumbai 400 036
Mob. 91 98202 81591

✱ Hugo Boss

Rs 4,000 onwards

Trendy, sleek and sophisticated, Hugo Boss offers clothes for the truly smart dressers. The swanky new showroom features suits, sports, formal and weekend wear in superior quality fabrics, and impeccable styles that cajole the crème of society. A lifestyle approach completed with high standard footwear and above-average belts and wallets, the trimmings prim the look with genuine leather. So drop by and soak the spirit as models swagger their way across the ramps on slim plasma screens here.

Hilton Towers
Nariman Point
Mumbai 400 021
Ph. 91 22 2287 1020/21

bhmumbai@binhendi.com

DAILY 10-9

Hum India

Rs 99 - 1,500

Label rats who love low prices have just found one of the best cheeses in town. Foreign labels such as Bebe, Zara, and Fendi are available here at very decent prices, ranging from nightwear and lingerie to party wear. Don't be intimidated by the messy, stacks of clothes in the shop, your patience is promised to be rewarded well here.

Khan Manzil
704 Linking Road
Near Pizza Hut
Khar (W)
Mumbai 400 052
Ph. 91 22 5699 8066
MAP1 54

humindia@vsnl.net

DAILY 10.30-10

Hurley's

Rs 2,000 onwards

Hurley's believe fashion is 'the science of geometry, colour and drapery, all rolled into one.' Popular for its bimonthly magazines on ethnic couture, Hurley's has recently expanded its forte to heavy Indian and indo-western wear for formal occassions. Coordinated with the colours of the upcoming season, the clothes here mix tradition with sublime style, all at accecptable prices.

116-117 Cama
Industrial Estate
Sun Mill Compound
Lower Parel
Mumbai 400 013
Ph. 91 22 2492 7352

hurleys@vsnl.com
www.hurleysmag.com

DAILY 10-6.30 (Sun closed)

Images

Rs 150 - 6,000

Handbags of every size and shape flash to mind when one thinks of this shop. Primarily made for functional use, the products here range from leather totes, to embroidered and

Marshall Apartments
97, August Kranti Marg
Opp. Cumbala Hill
Hospital, Kemps Corner
Mumbai 400 036

printed slings in cane and woven fabrics. The men's accessories and women's wallets embellished with zardozi, Kashmiri and gara work, stand out in their elegance, and make perfect matches for formal Indian outfits.

Ph. 91 22 2380 4399/ 2380 6900

DAILY 10-7.30 (Sun closed)

Inc. 5

Rs 595 - 4,450

Shoe-a-holics, step up. Here comes Inc. 5 which believes that style and comfort don't necessarily have to contradict each other. Concentrating on cuts rather than elaborate embellishments, the store's products range from beachy sandals in citrus colours to formal shoes with elegant fringes. Guess and Raspberry also strut their ways in here, while broad leather belts and beaded bags complete the swish look.

Breach Candy
Mumbai 400 026
Ph. 91 22 2361 8616

DAILY 10-9.30 (Sun closed)

India Emporium

Rs 500 - 1,00,000

India Emporium promises to drape its customers in the latest georgettes, crepes and chiffons with fancy sequin and resham work. A wide selection of lehengas and salwar kameezes in ready-made and unstitched materials are also available here, to suit every taste and budget. Situated in the hub of the sari and diamond trade, this store especially sparkles out to visiting NRI clients.

91 - A Pearl Mansion,
Maharshi Karve Marg,
Mumbai 400 020
Ph. 91 22 2201 2935/ 2200 2346

indiaemporium@hotmail.com

DAILY 11-8 (Sun closed)

India-Weaves

Prices on Request

Opened by Pheroza J. Godrej, one of Mumbai's leading art patrons, India-Weaves is a state of the art textile-furnishing store. Besides luxurious candles, cushion covers and dramatic drapes, the tiny store stocks extravagant silk delights – strictly for connoisseurs with no budgetary constraints.

Near Cymroza Art Gallery
Bhulabhai Desai Road
Mumbai 400 026
Ph. 91 22 2364 6418
MAP2 55

DAILY 11-8 (Sun closed)

Indian States

Rs 300 - 50,000

It is almost impossible to miss this Marine Lines staple that offers a range of silk saris,

Jorawar Bhuvan
93 Maharshi Karve Road
Mumbai 400 020

salwar kameezes and bridal wear to its clients. Popular for its embroidery work, the shop prides itself on its designer craftsmanship and variety of products. Ready-made westerns, indo-western kurtis and printed shawls can also be found at the top floor of the store.

Ph. 91 22 2200 1262/ 8989

indianstates@vsnl.com

DAILY 9.30-8.30

Indigo Nation

Rs 185 - 1,699

A dress-down version to Zodiac, Indigo Nation boasts of providing reasonably priced, high quality products. Business and formal shirts sit alongside trousers at this store, while its semiformal range, Scullers, flourishes with basic shirts in checked and striped designs. Classy indigos and soft pastels colour the flag of this nation.

reachhemal@hotmail.com

DAILY 10-9 (Sun closed)

Zarapkars, Senapati Bapat Marg, Dadar (W)
Mumbai 400 028
Ph. 91 22 2430 6273

115 Oomrigar Building
Opp. Crawford Market
L.T. Marg
Mumbai 400 003
Ph. 91 22 2342 5366/ 5633 6643

Colaba Causeway
Mumbai 400 039
Ph. 91 22 2202 0197

Lokhandwala Complex
Next to Dominoes Pizza
Andheri (W)
Mumbai 400 058
Ph. 91 22 2632 5755

Instyle

Rs 500 - 60,000

The hit-and-miss variety, this 20-year-old store has recently restricted itself to men's wear on a retrenchment note. Popular with visiting NRI clients, the store specializes in ethnic wear including sherwanis, kurta pyjamas and bandhani stoles. Blazers and suits are accessorized here with wallets, cuff links and ties from Zodiac and in-house brands.

instyle@powersurfer.net

DAILY 10.30-8

7 Napean Sea Road
Mumbai 400 036
Ph. 91 22 2369 1335/ 2364 0611, **MAP2 53**

Intouch Leather

Rs 310 onwards

The only store at InOrbit Mall in touch with swinging accessories, the shop strings a multitude of bags. Basic leather ones in a kaleidoscope of colours, along with a small range of trendy 'jelly Kellys' and beaded party bags can be spotted here. The unusual creations of French-Riviera-inspired tiffin boxes and denim totes with leather fringes are the shop's true stunners.

DAILY 10-10

L/3 Gr. Floor
InOrbit Mall Ind. (P). Ltd.
Mind - Space, Link Road
Malad (W)
Mumbai 400 064
Ph. 91 22 5640 6988

In-Urges

Rs 200 - 2,500

All you teeny girlies who have too small a savings account and too large an appetite for shopping...go ahead and indulge your urge here. Tucked away in a corner, this shop has heaps of cheap casual and party-wear clothing, tight ribbed tops, sleek halter necks and tangy trousers. Clothes are high on the fashion scale but low in quality, so be careful when you make your selection.

G-3
Chinoy Mansion
Inside Compound
Warden Road
Mumbai 400 036
Ph. 91 22 2368 5971

DAILY 11-8 (Sun closed)

IN XS

Rs 100 - 1,600

Spice up your wardrobe this season with chromatic bags to match your every outfit. Following the fashion trends abroad, IN XS has a range of bags for every age. Splashes of traffic-light reds, lemony yellows, blue denims and classic blacks and whites add to the scores here, along with shoes to match. Without doubt, a 'miss-not' destination for every missie who can never have her accessories in excess!

Kemp's Corner
Opp Shalimar Hotel
Mumbai 400 056
Ph. 91 22 5600 4573

DAILY 11-8.30 (Sun closed)

* Ishna

Rs 500 onwards

Avoid the hit-and-miss format of making a style statement, by shopping at this enigmatic store. Looking like a riot of colours with floral skirts, embroidered kurtis and trendy lehengas, Ishna specializes in the fusion look. Winding chappals, sequinned stoles and fancy handbags add to the fervour, while funky jackets for the hunky men particularly flex out. Spacious and vibrant, this store is what dreams are made of for the fashion diehards.

184 Sagar Fortune
Waterfield Road, Bandra
Mumbai 400 050
Ph. 91 22 2640 1002/08
MAP1 57

jewellery@ishnastore.com
www.ishnastore.com

DAILY 11-8.30 (Sun closed)

Istaa

Rs 300 - 3,000

This new addition to Bandra's plethora of fashion stores stands out for its warm wooden interiors and comfortable casual Indian wear. Kurtis and salwars in refreshing summery cotton handlooms and voiles hang on the racks, while ethnic art jewellery adorn brass showpieces. Easy-to-manage

13/14 Zarina CHS Ltd
S.V. Road, Bandra (W)
Mumbai 400 050
Ph. 91 22 2640 4233/
2640 4246

style with prices to match, Istaa is a hassle-free destination for the working woman of today.

info@istaa.com
www.istaa.com

DAILY 11-8.30 (Sun closed)

Istante

Rs 300 - 2,000

Floating racks display a variety of Indian, western, and fusion wear, at this cosy shop. Cheered with floral skirts, fuscia capris, trousers, and trendy tops, the clothes here are all set to serenade you. Belts, handbags and footwear join in, with sprite in this frolic parade, while the Indian counterparts of short kurtas, saris and indo-westerns fall behind in the zest spirit.

Shop No 7, Sagarika Apt
Opp. Palm Grove Hotel
Juhu, Mumbai 400 049
Ph. 91 22 2617 5923

instante_boutique@hotmail.com

DAILY 11-7.30 (Sun closed)

Ixtapa

Rs 600 onwards

A 'temple of style', for the hip and happening people, Ixtapa imports its faddish collection of unbranded clothes from Europe. With pulsating psychedelic shirts and fancy footwear, the men's range here doesn't fall short on the trend-o-meter either. A kinky line of pom-pom and net lingerie, along with other miscellanea makes Ixtapa an exciting place to start, while revamping one's wardrobe or dressing style.

1 Sea Palace
Juhu Tara Road
Next to Sea Princess Hotel
Juhu, Mumbai 400 049
Ph. 91 22 2660 6154/ 2660 5041, **MAP1 58**

ixtapa@vsnl.com

DAILY 10.30-8.30S (Sun closed)

J'aime

Rs 250 - 4,000

Bursting with hearts, 'you'll like' this hip, retro and flirty shop. Sashaying in skirts, discoing in denim, and cascading in kaftans, the clothes here are all set to join in, for a tantalizing tango. Knock-offs of the season's latest accessories at reasonable prices along with imported fashion wear, make this a popular rendezvous spot for young Romeos and Juliets of the area.

Gagangiri Co-op
Society Ltd
Bldg 'A' Shop No.104
Off Carter Road,
Khar (W)
Mumbai 400 052
Ph. 91 22 2605 0118

j_aime2003@yahoo.com

DAILY 12-8 (Sun closed)

Jaipur Bandhej

Rs 1,000 - 30,000

From the sand dunes of the desert to the urban jungle of Mumbai, this store brings traditional bandhanis and leheriyas in its myriad hues. Saris and lehengas are emblazed with embroidery and sequins in 'designer' ways; whereas other handicrafts include block-printed salwars and kota saris for casual wear. A safe option for the bridesmaid's mehendi dance as bandhanis never swing out of fashion.

Shop 7, Chandralok 'A',
97 Napean Sea Road,
Mumbai 400 026
Ph. 91 22 2368 6588

89, Maker Arcade,
G. D. Somani Road,
Cuffe Parade,
Mumbai 400 005
Ph. 91 22 2216 5620

DAILY 11-8 (Sun closed)

Jaipur Saree Kendra

Rs 350 - 25,000

Bringing the bright colours of Rajasthan alive, this alcove stocks a gamut of traditional outfits for women. This well-stocked shop boasts of ethnic garments embellished with tikki, gotapatti and sequin work. Dealing only in pure materials, the bandhani saris and block-printed cottons are ideal for daily use.

Shop No. 2 & 3
Beach Haven 2
Net to Hotel Palm
Grove, Juhu Tara Rd.
Mumbai 400 049
Ph. 91 22 2617 1640/
2617 2644

69/A Manisha Building
Napean Sea Rd
Mumbai 400 006

DAILY 10.30-8.30 (Sun closed)

James Ferriera

Rs 2,500 - 1,00,000

Working natural fibres in basic colours, James Ferriera's clothes are timeless classics with whimsical streaks of quirkiness. Creating eclectic garments with a special emphasis on trousseau wear, this designer makes Indian, fusion and western outfits after personal meetings with individual clients. An avant-garde couturier, James Ferriera believes in experimentation and bequeaths garments, fizzing with effervescence and fervour.

Khotachi Wadi
Gamdevi
Mumbai 400 007
Ph. 91 22 2388 7292
MAP2 59

BY APPOINTMENT ONLY

Jane Shilton

Rs 500 - 3,000

If making the style pages was never on your wish list, this store might be a good source for benign quality and functional handbags. Jane Shilton targets contemporary working women with basic bags in bigger sizes; while the smaller selection of trendier slings in coloured leathers bring accessories for the more adventurous.

3 Juhu Princess
Juhu Tara Road
Mumbai 400 049
Ph. 91 22 2614 0044

F-30 A Quorum
Phoenix Mills
Senapati Bapat Marg,
Lower Parel,
Mumbai 400 013
Ph. 91 22 2497 2860
MAP1 60

www.janeshilton.com

DAILY 11-8

Jashn

Rs 245 - 45,000

A carnival of colours, Jashn has a large variety of silk, cotton and Italian crepe saris along with unstitched salwar kameezes. Popular for its screen indigo and block-printed work, the shop's clothes rejoice in their Indian designs and floral prints. With unique feminine forms and high quality fabrics, clothes for every festival can be found here.

unithead@mshsaris.com

MON-FRI 10.30-8.30
SAT-SUN 10.30-9.30

MSH Saris Pvt. Ltd
207 Crystal Centre
Raheja Vihar, Powai
Mumbai 400 076
Ph. 91 22 2857 4413

A-8, R-Mall, L.B.S. Marg
Mulund (W)
Mumbai 400 080
Ph. 91 22 5598 8073/
5598 8074

F-18, InOrbit Mall
Mind Space, Link Road
Malad (W)
Mumbai 400 064
Ph. 91 22 5643 0664

Jewelart

Rs 75 - 5,000

An assortment of rings and earrings for women and unisex initial pendants and ID bracelets are available at this store. Supreme in quality, the products are traditional and hip, with ethnic silver sets going back in time and jelly and evil eye bracelets keeping up with current trends. A fairly priced jewel, this store promises to add a silver lining to any occasion.

avijewel@hotmail.com

DAILY 10.30-7.30 (Sun closed)

91 Bhulabhai Desai Road
Mumbai 400 036
Ph. 91 22 2367 6227/
2367 6301
Mob. 91 98205 13311
MAP2 B1

✷ Jolly

Rs 2,500 - 5,000

Here's another reason to go shoe shopping at The Oberoi. From flirtatious strappy sandals with corky heels to wow stilettos with leather trimmings, there is a real flair to the collections here. Neither too mainstream nor too offbeat, their accessories often steal the limelight; so come prepared to give your designer outfits some jolly good competition.

DAILY 10-8.30, SUN 11-5

F63/64 Oberoi
Shopping Arcade,
The Oberoi
Nariman Point
Mumbai 400 021
Ph. 91 22 2204 1230

Joolry

Rs 300 onwards

A true gem found just outside the frenzied Heera Panna market, this 'Joolry' shop sells swanky fashion jewels for the lunching ladies of Mumbai. A combination of elegant rings, earrings and pendants are found here, along with a voguish collection of diamante studded jelly wristbands and evil eye bracelets. With down-to-earth prices, this fashion shop sky rockets its customers to dazzling heights.

DAILY 11-8 (Sun closed)

G-13
Heera Panna Shopping
Arcade, Haji Ali
Mumbai 400 026
Ph. 91 22 2351 1628/
2351 1629

Joy Shoes

Rs 695 - 3,000

Recently redone, the 65-year-old shop proudly proclaims that 'M.F. Hussain, a barefoot artist has designed this shoe shop'. Dealing in leather accessories, Joy Shoes truly proves that quality does speak for itself. Although popular for its evening stilettos and bridal footwear collections, the shop's Kolhapuris and mojris are also making fashion waves abroad. Classic and trendy, this shop has joyfully edged its way onto the shopping lists of the ritzy.

The Taj Mahal Palace & Towers
Apollo Bunder
Mumbai 400 001
Ph. 91 22 2202 8696/ 2284 1227

munna@joyshoes.net

DAILY 10-7.30, SUN 11.30-7.30

Just Carnival

Rs 550 - 50,000

Specializing in groom's wear, Just Carnival also provides business and casual clothing for men. Offering a range of international brands, the shop stockpiles jeans, raingear and woollens, amongst others. With an exclusive studio dedicated to personal client meetings, here is a store with a perennial fashion carnival, where everyone is always invited.

39 Hill Road
Opp. Elco Market
Bandra (W)
Mumbai 400 050
Ph. 91 22 2640 7054/ 2642 8237

info@justcarnivalindia.com
www.justcarnivalindia.com

DAILY 10-9

Just Kids

Rs 100 - 1,000

A small store with a large variety of products, Just Kids has casual and party wear for kiddos up to 10 years. Stacked messily, the t-shirts, shorts, pants and jeans might look as (un-) appealing as your brat's wardrobe, but is worth rummaging through for some reasonable finds.

27 A
Tirupati Shopping
Bhulabhai Desai Road
Mumbai 400 026
Ph. 91 22 2490 2070
MAP2 62

DAILY 10.30-9 (Sun closed)

Just Maternity

Rs 300 onwards

When you are so full of happiness, the last thing you want to look is dull and drab. With its collection of casual clothes, with simple cuts and designs, Just Maternity helps 'moms-to-be' to look and feel good every day. From pants and capris to gowns and dungarees, all the garments here are comfortable in price and standard in quality.

Shop No. 4
Dilkoosha Building
5A Altamount Road
Opp. Bank of India
Mumbai 400 026
Ph. 91 22 2388 2122

DAILY 11-7 (Sun closed)

Just Moms

Rs 30 onwards

Dress your little wonder with this shop's cushy cotton clothing. Providing a range of items from capris to frilled dresses, the store also stacks shoes, caps and belts for infants up to the age of five. Popular for its cartoon character prints, this store is going to be a sure-hit with all Shrek and Spiderman fans.

Shop No. 2
Narendra Bhavan
51 Bhulabhai Desai Rd.
Mumbai 400 026
Ph. 91 22 2352 1400/
2351 7833, **MAP2 63**

DAILY 9.30-8.30

JVP

Rs. 650 - 7,000

Launched by Amitabh Bachchan, the designer prêt wear label, JVP from Kala Niketan surely made an entrance in style. Flowers and colour dominate this shop here, which offers clichéd but upmarket quality clothing. While the shop does stock skirts and pants, it is the expansive collection of women's shirts which really stand out. From clubwear shirts to casual cottons - JVP has much to offer.

Quorum Phoenix Mills
Senapati Bapat Marg,
Lower Parel,
Mumbai 400 013

DAILY 10-8 (Sun closed)

Kachins Clothing

Rs 85 - 2,000

Snatch the corporate spotlight with sharp suits, blazers and shirts by Kachins Clothing. Using imported fabrics, along with digital tailoring, Kachins promises its customers, supreme quality products with immaculate fits. Formerly catering to the middle-aged man, the shop has recently launched a new line of stylish evening wear for the younger generation too. Indian clothes can be ordered here also.

kachins1@vsnl.com
www.kachinsclothing.com

DAILY 9.30-8.30 (Sun closed)

59 Wodehouse Road
Colaba
Mumbai 400 005
Ph. 91 22 2218 9249/
2215 3141

Classic Corner
Shop No. 7/8
St Andrews Rd.
Opp. Holy Family
Hospital
Bandra (W)
Mumbai 400 050
Ph. 91 22 2643 3730/
2643 9525

Kala Niketan

Rs 150 onwards

It's a different world inside this store, with its seemingly endless supply of Indian clothing for both men and women. Windowing the widest collection of saris, the shop also kurtis stocks, salwar kameezes and bridal lehengas. Men can find sherwanis and kurta pyjamas here; while young girls can adorn themselves with the shop's astounding variety of imitation jewellery.

DAILY 9.30-7.30 (Sun closed)

95 Queens Road
Mumbai 400 020
Ph. 91 22 2200 5001
MAP2 64

Navyug, J.V.P.D Scheme
Vile Parle
Mumbai 400 056
Ph. 91 22 2611 5689

Juhu Scheme, V M Road,
Santacruz
Mumbai - 400 059

Kamdhenu

Rs 50 - 3,000

Enter this store and submerge yourself in a sea of bits and pieces. From saris and infant frocks to crystal earrings and TIGI shampoos, the products here provide real 'value for money' vendibles; for those who know what they are looking for, and a variety of options for those who don't. An accessible store, Kamdhenu carries a vast collection of household goodies as well for its regular customers.

99 Videocon House,
Napean Sea Road
Mumbai 400 006
Ph. 91 22 2362 0204/05/06

DAILY 9-9

✹ Karma Kola

Rs 425 - 1,600

High on trend, low on price, this fashion shop has got its kitsch and international collections just right. Lined on the two sides of the store; the 'Karma' section boasts of crushed skirts, citrus and acid-coloured tops, and junky jewellery while the 'Kola' range is inspired by international trends and pop culture. A comprehensive store with a global image, Karma Kola is a 'must-visit' destination for fashion fetishers who can never have enough fizz in their wardrobes!

Bajaj Niwas
Opp. CKP Club
Linking Road, Khar
Mumbai 400 052
Ph. 91 22 3096 1063/ 2804 0562, **MAP1 65**

kola@indiatimes.com

MON-SAT 11.30-9, SUN 2-9

Kaysons

Rs 100 - 30,000

When you wear a sari, you drape a thousand years of tradition around yourself. For years, Kaysons has been offering this tradition through its wide variety of saris and sherwanis. Today, a trendier and more glamorous store, Kayson also caters western outfits to the groovy hearted. Ranging from unique patchwork pants and halter tops to printed kurtis and evil-eye embellished kaftans, this age-old brigade, has much to offer and admire.

Stadium House
Veer Nariman Road
Churchgate
Mumbai 400 020
Ph. 91 22 2284 3422/ 2284 3259, **MAP2 66**

Moonstone Apartments
65 E Linking Road
Santacruz (W)
Mumbai 400 054
Ph. 91 22 5679 1152/ 2648 7619

kaysonssaris@hathway.com

DAILY 10.30-8.00 (Sun closed)

KBN

Rs 100 - 80,000

A pleasant whiff of perfumes envelopes you as you enter this expansive upmarket departmental store. Chic interiors coupled with clear demarcations of departments –

501 Linking Road, Khar,
Mumbai 400 052
Ph. 91 22 2646 5511/ 5695 4444, **MAP1 67**

men, women, children, and accessories – make KBN a shopping delight. Foreign labels such as Versus, Diesel and Guess are also available at this store.

kbn@vsnl.com

DAILY 11-9

Kimaya

Rs 5,000 onwards

The maya enamoured on to this store is for the purely gilded only. The enchantment of outfits' onstage range from dewy chiffon tops and decadent denim tunics to magnificent muu-muus and sanguine salwars, all in enthralling styles; with an imposing sequence of heavy-weight designer-names adding to the chimera. An expansive choice in the choicest of garments, Kimaya presents an indulgent ambience for brides-to-be and tinsel queens.

2, Asha Colony,
Juhu Tara Road,
Mumbai 400 049
Ph. 91 22 26606154
MAP1 68

hirani@kimayastudio.com
www.kimayastudio.com

DAILY 11-8 (Sun closed)

Kink

Rs 300 - 2,500

Brainchild of Gautam Hinduja, a former Channel [V] stylist, it's no surprise that Kink attracts the younger and trendier lot. Unbranded denims, shredded skirts and skimpy halters, imported from the Far East, make prices and quality reasonable with style overriding. Popular for its accessories, the handbags and shoes are the shop's true highlights; making this fashion warehouse a kinky alternative to branded shopping.

209, Waterfield Road
Bandra (W)
Mumbai 400 050
Ph. 91 22 5677
8093/8094, MAP1 69

DAILY 12-9, SUN 2.30-9

Kittens

Rs 190 - 750

Purr... Kittens provides a bright and bubbly source of extremely wearable children's footwear. On the racks is a comprehensive range of sandals, sports and formal shoes for children 10 months to 16 years. Special care is taken to ensure comfort and flexibility with supple soles, while a trendier selection includes sequins sandals for girls and closed boots for boys. Prance on to protect your little one's paws.

R Mall
LBS Marg, Mulund (W)
Mumbai 400 080
Ph. 91 22 5555 0904

Below Cumbala Hill
Bridge, Kemps Corner
Mumbai 400 036
Ph. 91 22 2387 2501/
2344 5650

Lokhandwala Complex
Kamdhenu Shop, Shop
No.55, Andheri (W)
Mumbai 400 058
Ph. 91 22 2631 2401

www.kittensworld.com

DAILY 10-9.30

Krishna Mehta

Rs 530 - 25,000

This shop showcases designer Krishna Mehta's splendid Indian and western clothing. With a passion for embroidery and natural fabrics, the men's clothes are kept basic; while the women's range is splashed with colours galore. Her western outfits are a must-see as well.

6 Quorum High Street
Phoenix Mill Compound
462 Senapati Bapat Marg, Lower Parel
Mumbai 400 013

krishnamehta@vsnl.com
www.krishnamehta.com

DAILY 11-8

L'vista

Prices on Request

A blend of luxury and practicality, Shahnaz Mahimtura's L'vista is a lifestyle store offering accessories and artwork. Handmade furniture with details of wood sticks and bamboo reeds teamed with leather, glass, cane, abaca weaves and unique polishes invoke a Balinese spirit here, while the sofas, cabinets, reclining chairs, and beds speak of luxurious comfort. A collection of paintings from Yusuf Arrakal, amongst other artists also finds a space in this shop.

Phoenix Mills
Shop No. 9, 10, 11
462 Senapati Bapat Marg
Lower Parel
Mumbai 400 013
Ph. 91 22 5660 4541

MON-SAT 10.30-8, SUN 12.30-8

Lacoste

Rs 650 - 5,200

The crocodile logo has revolutionized a long way from the signature polo and 'petit pique' jersey knits to windcheaters and eyewear. Lacoste's formal, casual and sportswear gets softer with every wash; providing casual elegance in bold colours and uncompromising quality. Leather belts, wallets, ties and travel bags available at the shop, also make timeless gift items.

65 Breach Candy
Mumbai 400 026
Ph. 91 22 2361 8616
MAP2 70

Reham Mansion
Shop No. 1A
Colaba Causeway
Mumbai 400 039
Ph. 91 22 22851 7974

Phoenix Mills,
462, Senapati Bapat Marg, Lower Parel
Mumbai 400 013

DAILY 11-8

Young Hearts, 5/270 Linking Road, Bandra
Mumbai 400 050, Ph. 91 22 2643 9566

The Oberoi, Treasures, Shop No. 14, Nariman Point
Mumbai 400 021, Ph. 91 22 2288 1017

Shop No C213-214-28, Pt. M.M. Malviya Road
Haji Ali, Mumbai 400 034, Ph. 91 22 2495 5108

✷ Lady Grace

Rs 100 - 2,000

Immerse yourself in affordable grandeur at Lady Grace. Devdas-style juda pins, kundan necklaces, ornate waistbands and jhumka key-chains, make you feel like a princess; while an array of bangles set with crystals, pearls and diamantes, spoil you for choice. The contemporary end coos with a range of trendy earrings, where colourful anklets and funky wigs allure sassy supporters. Visit this Lady while preparing for an outstation wedding or when simply sprucing up your feminine boudoir.

144, VP Road
Near Sikka Nagar
Mumbai 400 004
Ph. 91 22 2388 1253
MAP2 71

DAILY 10.30-8.40 (Sun closed)

Lawman

Rs 495 - 1,495

Denim seems to be the law with this officer. A part of the Killer group, the store stocks casual wear for men. Denims in different colours, blasts and washes stack the racks in the form of jeans, jackets and half and full-sleeves shirts; while synthetic-mix trousers and cotton shirts from their label, 'Integriti', strengthen the enforcement.

Citi Centre
SV Road
Goregaon (W)
Mumbai 400 062
Ph. 91 22 2876 2731

DAILY 10.30-9.30 (Thurs Closed)

Lāzāree

Rs 250 - 10,000

Celebrate every tradition of India at Lâzaree with saris from around the country including Banarsi weaves, Bangalore silks, Kanjivarams and Patolas in a spectrum of colours. A collection of embroidered modern saris and salwar kameezes from Kolkata are available here. A relatively pleasant ambience in an otherwise chaotic neighbourhood, Lâzaree assures service with a smile.

364/A Bedekar Sadan
NC Kelkar Road
Dadar (W)
Mumbai 400 028
Ph. 91 22 2430 8128

www.lazaree.com

DAILY 9.30-8.30 (Mon Closed)

Le Bijou

Rs 50 - 5,000

This hole-in-the-wall with trinkets and jewels galore, manages to make its way onto every fashion magazine on the racks. Plastic earrings, cascading metallic necklaces, and funky stick-on tattoos assure to gild your look with spunky funk; while the striking pom-pom net sets and other kinky lingerie, seduce quite another dimension to the store's bijou character.

Mahavir Bhuvan
37 Hill Road,
Opp. Elco Market
Bandra (W)
Mumbai 400 050
Ph. 91 22 2644 3473/
2056 0186, **MAP1 72**

DAILY 9.30-9

Leather Farm

Rs 2,500 - 6,000

If you are searching for Hrithik Roshan's 'Kaho Na Pyaar Hai' leather jacket finesse, start counting your steps to this store. A fashion-savvy shop, the garments here are stylized in line with latest fashion trends. From asymmetric suede skirts to biker-style jackets, you can be assured of finding your leather style potion here.

F/96 H.C. Level Oberoi Tower
Nariman Point
Mumbai 400 021
Ph. 91 22 2285 6654

DAILY 10.30-7 (Sun closed)

Leather Touch

Rs 150 - 5,000

No surprises here, it's just leather available in all its utilities. Wallets, belts and travel accessories fill the shop's shelves, while bold coloured leather jackets and pants are customized as per personal preferences. Though nothing extraordinary, the shop adds yet another option to the lavish leather buffet on offer at the arcade.

F12/F90 Oberoi
Shopping Arcade,
Nariman Point,
Mumbai 400 021
Ph. 91 22 2282 5720

mvaljee@rediffmail.com

DAILY 11.30-7.30 (Sun closed)

Lee

Rs 395 onwards

Stamped for perfection, Lee offers quality clothes that aspire to take you 'back to the streets'. The new 'X-Line' provides a button-fly range in exciting cuts and diverse denim flavours, whereas the 101 collection presents the vintage look inspired by cowboy days. The brand's small 'Leesures' line offers comfort-wear shirts and trousers; all serving to dress-up those chilled out soda-sipping-afternoons.

Dhun-Abad Building
Junc. Warden Rd &
Napean Sea Rd
Mumbai 400 026
Ph. 91 22 2368 5306

Shop13,
Rahem Mansion
Colaba Causeway
Mumbai 400 005
Ph. 91 22 2284 1467
MAP2 73

250A, Linking Road, Khar (W), Mumbai 400 050
Ph. 91 22 2644 1783

Prospect Chamber, 315 Dr. DN Road, Fort
Mumbai 400 023, Ph. 91 22 2282 0150/ 2284 4598

DAILY 11-8

Levi's

Rs. 1,199-4,000

Believe it or not, Levi Strauss made the first pair of button-fly Original 501s in 1853, and in the process revolutionized clothing style. Levi's offers its patrons a variety of innovative fits and trendy washes in jeans. The brand also has a smart-casual collection of college bags and caps; while basic tees, cotton capris and

Cusrow Baug
Colaba Causeway
Mumbai 400 005
Ph. 91 22 2284 0733

Next to Royal Chemist,
New Marine Lines
Mumbai 400 020,
Ph. 91 22 2200 3483

jackets add a diverse flavour to this denim dreamland.

originallevistore@yahoo.com
www.levis.com

DAILY 10.30-9

Prospect Chamber , 315 Dr. DN Road Fort,
Mumbai 400 023, Ph. 91 22 2282 0150/ 2284 4598

Shop No.1, Nalini Apartments
Linking Road, Khar (W)
Mumbai 400 052
Ph. 91 22 2600 1616
MAP1 74

Libas

Rs 350 - 18,000

A small shop specializing in made-to-order men's evening wear, Libas offers commendable quality clothing at well proportioned prices. Focusing on the subtle look with earthy colour combinations, the churidar kurtas available here are classy and understated. Also available in westerns are the zipper and three-button jackets along with waistcoats which run along the same restrained themes of the store.

riyaz_ganji@hotmail.com

Shop Here Shopping Mall, Green Ville Apts.
Shop No. 12, 1st Floor, Lokhandwala Complex
Andheri (W), Mumbai 400 053
Ph. 91 22 3091 4399/ 3091 0995
libas@vsnl.com
www.libasindia.com

DAILY 10.30-9, DAILY 10-10.30 (Andheri)

Sukh Shanti No.2
19 Dr. G. Deshmukh Marg
Cumballa Hill
Peddar Road
Mumbai 400 026
Ph. 91 22 2352 5145

Lifestyle

Rs 20 - 60,000

A multi-storeyed departmental store, Lifestyle has much to offer its patrons of all generations. Starting with infants, the store keeps branded clothes and accessories to suit every occasion and personality. Loaded with goodies, this store can add some affordable style to your life.

phx@lifestylestores.com

DAILY 10.30-9.30

639 Runwal Arcade, Lal Bahadur Shashtree Marg
Mulund (W), Mumbai 400 080

Phoenix Mills
462 Senapati Bapat Marg
Lower Parel
Mumbai 400 013
Ph. 91 22 5666 9200/ 9209

InOrbit Mall
Goregaon Malad Link Road, Off S.V. Road
Malad (W)
Mumbai 400 064
Ph. 91 22 5675 4277

Lilliput

Rs 295 - 800

Capris, skirts, t-shirts, jeans and jackets... this store racks clothes to dress the little people we love. A variety of styles in cottons for ages 10 months until 11 years is displayed here. Pleasant colours with just the right amount of trimmings make perfect garments for dolling up your Lilliputians, before sending them off to

Nirmal Lifestyle Mall
Mulund
Mumbai 400 080
Ph. 91 22 3450 3618

InOrbit Mall, Malad
Mumbai 400 064
Ph. 91 22 2303 5409

kick a ball, splash a puddle or simply to charm a friend.

Lilliput_nls@rediffmail.com

DAILY 11-8

Centre-1, Vashi,
Mumbai 400 703
Ph. 91 22 3109 3923

Atrium, Link Road,
Bandra,
Mumbai 400 050
(Opening Soon)

Live-in Store

Rs 500.- 1,000

A combination of affordability, youth and urban appeal, this store provides a comfy range of jeans that no college student would mind slipping into. A collection of smart-casual shirts, chinos and khakis available are affordable options for those who mix business with pleasure; while faded denim jackets and washed jeans please the cooler, unruffled lot. Fabrics used are 100 per cent cotton to ensure live-in comfort.

DAILY 10.30-10

R Mall,
LBS Marg
Mulund
Mumbai 400 080
Ph. 91 22 5598 0193

Centre 1, Vashi
Mumbai 400 703
Ph. 91 22 2781 2328

Lladro

Rs 5,000 - 17,00,000

'We want our works to be elegant, expressive, to ooze life and have feelings,' say the founding brothers of this porcelain-dream-maker, very much living up to their words. The artwork here needs no introduction, renowned for their fluid shapes depicting mythical characters and portraits of daily life, each piece has its own story to tell. Delicate and elegant, the sculptures here are sentimental, neo-romantic in style and masterpieces of design.

noopur.chablani@spaindia.com
www.lladro.com

DAILY 11-7.30 (Sun closed)

16/17 Om Chambers
Kemps Corner
August Kranti Marg
Mumbai 400 036
Ph. 91 22 2368 6374/75
MAP2 **75**

Lord & Taylor

Rs 800 - 7,500

Although known for gents tailoring, Lord & Taylor also offers suiting and shirting services to its esteemed clients. The store provides exclusive suit lengths from all leading Indian mills, as well as imported fabrics, to make precision tailored quality products. Shirts from Zodiac help to furnish the corporate ensemble.

DAILY 10.30-7.45 (Sun closed)

29 Sea Castle Building
Chowpatty Seaface,
Mumbai 400 007
Ph. 91 22 2368 2335/36
MAP2 **76**

Lord's

Rs 190 - 2,990

A haven for footwear in all shapes and sizes – but not the kind that fetishes are made of.

Expect to find reflex-zone slip-ons to rejuvenate your sole, office shoes that consent the corporate climb and Reebok sneakers that make you jump; at this one-stop-family-shoe-shop. A collection completed with nearly every possible kind of hoof, Lord's will service your footy desires.

DAILY 10-8.30 (Sun closed)

6C Ama House, Strand Cinema Lane
Mumbai 400 005
Ph. 91 22 2288 1415

Metro House, Colaba Causeway
Mumbai 400 005
Ph. 91 22 2230 7597/ 2285 1928

254, Carnac Road,
Opp G.T.Hospital,
Near Crawford Market,
Mumbai 400 002
Ph. 91 22 2208 7136

131, Belram Bhawan,
Grant Road,
Mumbai 400 007
Ph. 91 22 2307 1619
MAP2 77

534 Linking Road,
Mumbai 400 050
Ph. 91 22 2648 2876

Louise Philippe

Rs 99 - 10,000

Stripes, checks, and plaids, are some of the designs you will see here. Primarily serving the white-collared gentry, Louise Philippe's shirts, trousers and suit sets, come in basic colours; indulging professionalism with a hint of style. Accessories include linen ties, belts and cuff links, while a small selection of casual wear sustains t-shirts and half-sleeve shirts.

lpturnerroad@satyam.net.in

DAILY 10.30-8.45

187 Turner Road,
Bandra (W),
Mumbai 400 050
Ph. 91 22 2643 2642

Louis Vuitton

Prices on Request

Add this store to your wish list as you blow out the candles this year with haute French fashion now available in the high streets of Mumbai. Providing a blue-ribbon collection of signature leather luggage and accessories, LV is a much-celebrated name with the pink of the society. Spelling exuberance, this brand takes effervescent style to the pedestal of world-class quality.

www.vuitton.com

DAILY 10-9 (Sun closed)

The Taj Mahal Hotel,
Apollo Bunder
Mumbai 400 001
Ph. 91 22 5665 3366

Madame

Rs 125 - 1,000

Jog in Madame and join the active girl's league. Fashionable sports gear including tracks, sporty spaghettis and trendy rugby-tops win the race here hands down, while formal trousers, skirts, and denims make their way to the finish line. Strong on tees with brave slogans, this shop is

Lokhandwala Complex,
Andheri (W),
Mumbai 400 053
Ph. 91 22 5693 1399

for those who believe that 'winning is the name of the game'.

madrajesh@rediffmail.com

DAILY 11-9.30

Maheka Mirpuri/ IV Life Fashion

Prices on Request

Energetic colours flavour the palette of this young designer making fitted backless kurtas, trendy shararas, and embroidered hipsters for women; while men are treated with crystal embellished linen kurtas. Bold and offbeat belts and neckpieces, chiffon pouches with sequin peripherals and twisted rope slings with crystal tassels and bugle beads, make the accessories exciting. Fusing designs for semi-formal occasions and bridal evenings, IV Life Fashion spills on the right amount of shimmer to tease all damsels.

469, Veer Savarkar Marg
Prabhadevi
Mumbai 400 025
Ph. 91 22 2432 7777
MAP2 78

maheka@mahekamirpuri.com
www.mahekamirpuri.com

BY APPOINTMENT ONLY

Malabar Boutique

Rs 350 - 5,000

Lavish yet modest, this Malabar lifestyle boutique has a beautiful display of antiques, home furnishing and fashion accessories. A plethora of hand-crafted items include silver trinkets, silk fabrics, stoles and saris, all stylishly enveloped in ornate woodwork; while its raw silk jackets, linen shirts and Italian tunics convey elegance with class.

The Taj Mahal Hotel,
Room 131, Heritage
Wing,, Apollo Bunder
Mumbai 400 001
Ph. 91 22 2202 9703

dimple_a@hotmail.com

DAILY 10-7 (Sun closed)

Man O' Man

Rs 495 - 1,500

You would not expect to find a clean and sophisticated store amidst the confusion of Crawford Market, but Man O' Man, will you be surprised. Providing a variety of business wear for men, the shop also houses party tops, jeans and windcheaters; while a range of branded undergarments adds to the paraphernalia.

Crawford Market
Mumbai 400 002
Ph. 91 22 2305 2774/
2343 6030

DAILY 10.30-9 (Sun closed)

Mango/MNG

Rs 390 - 28,000

Recreating every season's look before anyone else can, it's no surprise that Mango has its 'addicts'. This double-storeyed showroom has a wide selection of clothes ranging from office suits and disco-drapes to carefree capris and breezy bikinis. Funky belts, hip handbags, feline footwear and stylish eyewear are amongst the accessory bestsellers offered by this Spanish label. Bringing international fashion to Indian shores, the Mango ripens just right every season.

Crossroads
28, Pt M.M. Malviya Rd.
Haji Ali
Mumbai 400 034
Ph. 91 22 5662 7292

MON-FRI 10-9, SAT-SUN 10-9.30

Manish Arora/ Fish Fry

Rs 2,950 - 13,950

The clouds, psychedelic bongs and blue crystal chandelier set just the right mood for Manish Arora's kitsch, funky and eclectic style. From linen salwars with crushed dupattas to his prêt 'Fish Fry' line, the designer's shop is a flamboyant riot of colours. Signature khadi-printed kurtis, ultra-short cheerleader skirts, corset tops and funky tunics, are made for the bold and beautiful; while the very wearable Indian collection bridges somewhere between fun and funk.

The Courtyard,
S.P. Centre
41/44
Minoo Desai Marg
Colaba
Mumbai 400 005
Ph. 91 22 5638 5464/65

alpa@threeclothingco.com

DAILY 11-8

Marco

Rs 500 - 15,000

Catering to men more of its own age, this store looks to spruce up wardrobes with classic western and Indian wear. Using expensive interlining materials, the shop specializes in made-to-measure suits, while its embroidered sherwanis, darbaris and kurtas are popular as well. Thanks to their comfortable fits and prices, the linen shirts, trousers and silk ties deserve a second look.

177 J. Dadaji Road
Opp. Ganga Jamuna
Cinema, Tardeo
Mumbai 400 007
Ph. 91 22 2380 4354
MAP2 78

marcofashion@vsnl.com

DAILY 9.30-8 (Sun closed)

Marco Ricci

Rs 495 - 4,975

This established Italian brand has only recently opened its first exclusive store in Mumbai. With a prime focus on men's footwear, this store includes a subtle and ultra-durable collection of well-crafted shoes. Other styles

F27 InOrbit Malls -
Mindspace, Link Road,
Malad (W)
Mumbai 400 064
Ph. 91 22 5643 0399

range from suede moccasins and black ankle-length boots to ruffled leather formals; while the belts, wallets, and sunglasses serve to add spunk to the accessories bandwagon.

info@marcoricci.net
www.marcoricci.net

DAILY 10.45-9.30

Marks & Spencer

Rs 1,150 - 11,700

This British store needs no introduction. The shop's casual Blue Harbour range keeps shirts, cargos, and chinos for men and women, while its formal SP collection includes classy shirts and trousers for the same. Spots, stripes and floral prints in understated colours are the mantra of the clothes, while the satin night-suits, lingerie and jelly shoes stroke a delicate whisper to the store.

Skyzone Block 2
Phoenix Mills
462 Senapati Bapat Marg
Lower Parel
Mumbai 400 013
Ph. 91 22 5666 9807/ 5666 9808

mnspsm@planetsportsindia.com

DAILY 11-9.30

C 001 Ground Floor, 28 Pandit M.M. Malviya Road, Tardeo, Mumbai 400 034
Ph. 91 22 5660 4664

U 48/49/50, InOrbit Mall, Link Road
Malad (W), Mumbai 400 064, Ph. 91 22 5643 0426

✻ Master Pieces - Galerie de Designe

Rs 500 onwards

This lifestyle store is like a walk through an elaborately decorated English house–the rooms are dressed according to themes, complete with furniture, drapes, lampshades, upholstery and accessories, mostly in floral designs. A range of carpets from Jaipur, candle stands from Kolkata, bamboo lamps and plants from Bangkok, blown-glass from Pune, and mosaic vases from Ferozabad, can be seen here. Jam-packed spaces include wrought-iron accessories, Royal Doulton crockery, table linen, bedspreads, wallpapers, charcoal drawings and paintings to mention a few. Definitely worth a visit!

Jony Castle
Khatau Road
Off 92/98
Wodehouse Road
Colaba
Mumbai 400 005
Ph. 91 22 2216 1093

DAILY 11-7 (Sun closed)

Mayuri

Rs 700 - 50,000

Just like a peacock flaunting its plumes, this reputed store proudly displays its wide collection of lehengas and saris for women. Although most popular for its custom made bridal wear, Mayuri also seethes a-lined, fishtail and mermaid-cut skirts, perfect for fizzy

Shop No. 8
Vaishali Shopping Centre
J.V.P.D Scheme
Next to Sahakari
Bhandar, Vile Parle (W)
Mumbai 400 049
Ph. 91 22 2610 2088
MAP1 80

cocktail parties. With saris by Anamika Khanna demanding to be noticed, the less pompous lot stand coyly in their reasonable prices.

91 Parul Mansion
Queens Road
Mumbai 400 020
Ph. 91 22 2200 3658

www.mayurisaris.com

DAILY 11-8 (Sun closed)

ME – Furniture & Beyond

Prices on Request

Jointly owned by designer Mustafa Eisa and Birla Lifestyles, this store imports contemporary furniture from China. The sprawling showroom includes metal framed and leather lounger-cum-sofa and chaise-cum-stool combinations in cotton, along with beds and dressers. Although priced on the higher side, ME is a good destination for outdoor furniture as well.

Paragon Condominium
G-Block, Opposite
Century Mills, Worli
Mumbai 400 013
Ph. 91 22 5663 3666 / 3999, **MAP2 81**

DAILY 10.30-7.30

Me 'N' Moms

Rs 20 - 1,500

Mommies and their tiny tots can play peek-a-boo at this store, which has a separate play area for kids. This playground also displays a variety of bright casual clothing for kids, along with dungarees, frocks and night suits for maternity wear. With walls painted in bright lemon green, the happy store has a separate shoe shop, one step away, with tiny shoes for twiddling toes.

7/ 11 Amrapali
Shopping Centre
V.M. Road
Near Kala Niketan
J.V.P.D
Mumbai 400 049
Ph. 91 22 2611 3630/ 2617 8115, **MAP1 82**

DAILY 10-9

Mehendi

Rs 500 - 2,000

Decorate your body with colourful outfits from this store that claims to have the latest designs in kurtis, salwar kameezes and lehengas. Made of synthetic materials, the clothes are available in varying styles and average quality. Asking for reasonable prices in return, the shop can have customers from every income bracket 'sajo-ing and racho-ing' here.

4 Hotel Jewel of
Chembur
1st Road, Opp. B.M.C.
Chembur
Mumbai 400 071
Ph. 91 22 2528 0205

chembur@vsnl.com
www.chembur.com/mehendi

TUE-SUN 10-10

Mélange

Rs 1,500 onwards

Chime in, through the wrought-iron door into this world of mélanges: of vintage with contemporary, of chai with Kahlua and of devis

33 Altamount Road,
Mumbai 400 026
Ph. 91 22 2385 4492
MAP2 83

and divas. The theme is recurrent as fusion wear dominates with home-spun fibres in western silhouettes, traditional embroideries in edgy cuts and structured yet free spirited garments. Drizzling in some of the prêt-a-porter, are Savio Jon and Vivre, while the heavier downpours in the traditional collection come from Kimono and Rohit Bal.

melange@vsnl.com
www.melangeworld.com

DAILY 10-7 (Sun closed)

Men's Boulevard

Rs 2,000 - 75,000

An avenue dedicated to men's wear, this one-stop-shop for men is a hot favourite with the filmi crowd. Ethnic men's wear includes kurta pyjamas, sherwanis and crushed dupattas to complete the Punjab-da-puttar-look; while formal, business-casual and weekend shirts with trousers, please the more urban kind. In addition, suit sets can be custom-tailored from a selection of fabrics available here.

DAILY 10.30-10

26/17 InOrbit Mall,
Malad (W),
Mumbai 400 064
Ph. 91 22 5643 0406/ 040

Bhagwan's
Santacruz (W)
Mumbai 400 049
Ph. 91 22 26493468

Grand Hyatt Plaza
Santacruz (E)
Mumbai 400 054
MAP1 84

Metro

Rs 290 - 70,000

It is a reviving breeze of fresh air to enter this huge, air-conditioned flagship shoe store amongst the hustle-bustle of Colaba Causeway. This store offers a variety of footwear, from casual flip-flops, and beaded party sandals, to Swarovski-studded boots by Azeem Khan! Dealing in Hidesign handbags, and wallets, the shop also provides its own collection of acceptable quality leather accessories.

DAILY 10-10

534, Linking Road, Bandra, Mumbai 400 052
Ph. 91 22 26492899

Studio M, 532, Linking Road, Bandra, Mumbai 400 052
Ph. 91 22 26040972

Sagar Avenue, Opp. Shoppers' Stop, Andheri (W)
Mumbai 400 058, Ph. 91 22 26250512

113, S.V. Rd, Opp. Malad Shopping Centre
Mumbai 400 064, Ph. 91 22 28800987

Metro House
Colaba Causeway,
Mumbai 400 001
Ph. 91 22 5656 0444
MAP2 85

262, L.T. Road
Crawford Market
Mumbai 400 002
Ph. 91 22 2209 3668

Matru Chhaya
Grant Road
Mumbai 400 007
Ph. 91 22 2385 0311

3/5 Khodadad Circle
Dadar T.T
Mumbai 400 014
Ph. 91 22 24144651

77, M. G. Road
Ghatgopar (E)
Mumbai 400 077
Ph. 91 22 25169068

Milap

Rs 500 - Rs 50,000

Adding to the long list of sari shops, Milap has a mix of every kind of colour combination and design that comes to mind. With products designed by in-house artists, the store boasts

360 K.N. Building Road
Matunga (C.R.)
Mumbai 400 019
Ph. 91 22 2416 6364/65
Mob. 98203 27775
MAP2 86

of a diverse range of traditional and stylish drapery. Catering to women, young and old, this sea of fairly priced products brings together customers from varied economy brackets.

milapsaris@rediffmail.com
www.milapworld.com

TUE-SUN 9.30-9

Millionaire

Rs 1,500 onwards

Proudly announcing its target audience, Millionaire is most popular for groom's wear and its club and executive ranges. From classic looking suits to embroidered button- down sherwanis, the shop uses imported materials and embellishes them traditionally. Mojris and dupattas complete the Rajput attires here, while safaas and stoles serve to furnish the regalia.

Kemps Corner
Mumbai 400 026
Ph. 91 22 2382 5555
MAP2 87

30 Juhu Tara Road
Mumbai 400 049
Ph. 91 22 2660 4243

manager@millionairebombay.com
www.millionairebombay.com

DAILY 10.30-9.30 (Sun closed)

Mogra

Rs 150 - 1,20,000

A classy showroom with faux fur carpets, Mogra believes in encouraging new talent. With its primary focus on Indian and western prêt collections, the shop also flaunts some outstanding miscellanea in footwear, stoles and funky handbags. Showcased at the store's rear end is a small but truly exquisite collection of trendy imitation and real jewellery, making this modish store an inviting fashion aphrodisiac.

No. 10 Quorum,
1st floor,
High Street Phoenix,
462 Senapati Bapat Marg,
Lower Parel,
Mumbai 400 013
Ph. 91 22 3097 1300/30

mograstyle@yahoo.co.in

DAILY 11-8.30

Moksh

Rs 150 - 1250

Nirvana is not too far away when designers Ritu Kumar and Pallavi Rajdev get together to present a prêt collection at extremely affordable prices. The indo-chic look gets a boost with chromatic crushed skirts, kitschy sequinned kurtas and spaghetti tops while wooden earrings, beaded anklets and jhola bags furnish the gypsy look with an upbeat sprite.

21st Road
Near Khane Khaas
Bandra (W)
Mumbai 400 050
Ph. 91 22 2649 2010

DAILY 11-7.30

✹ Mont Blanc

Rs 4,000 onwards

This world-renowned brand carries classy accessories such as leather belts, wallets, silver cuff links, eyewear and signature pens. The perfect place to shop for a 'black-tie' event, or a family heirloom, Mont Blanc can make a gift truly memorable through personalized inscription. Boasting of superlative craftsmanship, the shop's accessories are a definite style statement, while ladies can look swish in the brand's latest collection of leather wallets and accessories.

The Taj Mahal Hotel
Apollo Bunder
Mumbai 400 001
Ph. 91 22 22852151

anna@entrackonline.com

DAILY 10-10

Moon River

Rs 1,500 onwards

Glass vases in every shape and size can be found here. Minimalist and classy, the theme here is refined yet restrained. You can pick up some great décor ideas by the display here, for instance float lemons in a huge cylindrical glass vase instead of flowers, you'll get a zest of colour, the serenity of still water and an avant-garde design!

The Courtyard
41/44 Minoo Desai
Marg, Colaba
Mumbai 400 005
Ph. 91 22 5638 5460/61

DAILY 10.30-7.30

Morgan

Rs 1,295 onwards

All you fashion-struck chicas, listen up. Morgan brings fashion to India all the way from Paris just for you. From casual t-shirts, to sophisticated formal outfits, everything here comes in tight cuts and bright colours, and of course, lots and lots of attitude. Mostly made with Lycra, the clothes cling on to your body for dear life, and only ask to be strutted around and admired in response. So for a groovy look, make sure you vroom in!

C - 003 Crossroads,
Pt. M. M. Malviya Marg
Haji Ali
Mumbai 400 034
Ph. 91 22 5660 4668/69

morgan@apgroupindia.com

DAILY 10-8.30

✹ Moss

Rs 800 - 6,000

You will not find sarongs at this 'by the beach' store, which showcases designer bags and shoes by the likes of Priyadarshini Rao and Deepika Sanghi. Although focusing on large slings with a French Riviera feel about them, the shop also

15 A, Union Park
Khar (W)
Mumbai 400 052
Ph. 91 22 3095 9405
MAP1 88

has a line of impeccably finished smaller bags that would add a zesty twang to any outfit. So roll over here, to gather some Moss.

DAILY 10-8

Ms. Banjaran

Rs 295 - 3,000

Much in sync with its name, Ms. Banjaran epitomizes the Indian gypsy look. Specializing in ethnic wear, the salwar kameezes, dupattas and chaniya cholis are made in silk and cotton fabrics, dyed with traditional bandhani. For a reasonable dandiya-night outfit, with quality to match, prance over to this rural-ragged shop.

2, Oberoi Shopping Centre,
The Oberoi,
Nariman Point,
Mumbai 400 021
Ph. 91 22 2283 4521

banjaran@email.com

DAILY 11-8 (Sun closed)

MTV Factory Outlet

Rs 295 - 1,195

For all mothers tired of watching their uber-trendy 15-year-olds making deliberate rips in their last pair of 'decent' jeans, this store provides the perfect solution. Not only does it offer a collection of funky pants (with ripped pockets of course), it also brings together a wide array of casual clothing, for all its cool clients. So stop by to lose youself in a sea of bright colours that could only be perpetuated by the brand that is MTV.

41 Good House Keeping (Pvt.) Ltd.
New Marine Lines
Mumbai 400 020

DAILY 10-8 (Sun closed)

Mykraft

Rs 200 - 1,200

Girlies with attitude, chin up, it's dress up time. Pretty flowers and garden bugs enthuse an energetic burst of colours here, on clothes that ensure the season's most fashionable styles for ages three months to 14 years. While girls can gloat gleefully with their reinvented wardrobes, parents watch out; the outfits might leave your little daughters looking way older than their age.

R Mall, LBS Marg,
Mulund (W),
Mumbai 400 080
Ph. 91 22 5555 4120
MAP1 89

Veer Savarkar Marg,
Prabhadevi,
Mumbai 400 025
Ph. 91 22 2422 4625

mykraft@vsnl.com
www.mykraftkids.com

DAILY 11.30-9 (Mulund)
TUE-SUN 10.30-8.30 (Prabhadevi)

Nagani's

Rs 50 onwards

Mind your step; you've just walked into one of Mumbai's oldest labyrinth of a store. From infant wear and handbags to jewellery and greeting cards, the merchandise here takes care of all your shopping requirements. Though not a style potion, this shop offers a convenient one-stop-shop for basics at thumbs-up prices.

MON-THURS 10.30-8.30
FRI-SUN 10.30-9.30

531 Linking Road,
Bandra,
Mumbai 400 052
Ph. 91 22 2605 9911/20, **MAP1 90**

Nagma's

Rs 195-3,000

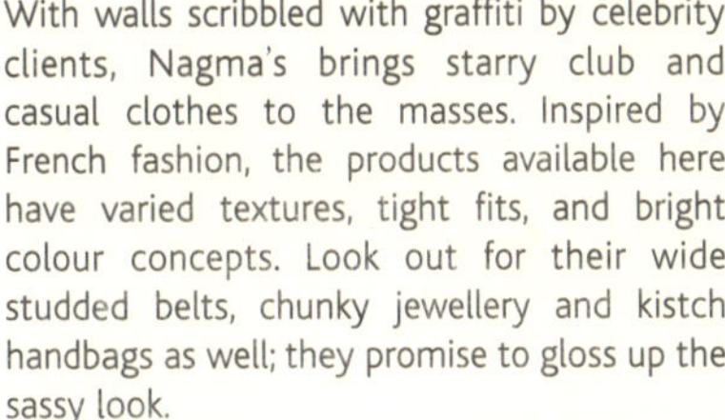

With walls scribbled with graffiti by celebrity clients, Nagma's brings starry club and casual clothes to the masses. Inspired by French fashion, the products available here have varied textures, tight fits, and bright colour concepts. Look out for their wide studded belts, chunky jewellery and kistch handbags as well; they promise to gloss up the sassy look.

nagmasjm@hotmail.com

DAILY 10-10.30 (Sun closed)

1 Venus, Hill Road
Bandra (W)
Mumbai 400 050
Ph. 91 22 2640 2589/ 2640 2564, **MAP1 91**

Naina's

Rs 1,500 onwards

True happiness lies in getting double of what you paid for; especially if it's designer wear. Specializing in reversible kurtis, Naina's has made a fairly new entry into the fashion fraternity. Warmly welcomed, the boutique's prêt line swishes sequinned corsets, Spanish blouses, and unique looking achkans, while its haute couture boasts of heavily embellished traditional outfits. So, to add a twinkle to your eye and a sparkle to your look, head straight here.

DAILY 10-8

Bhulabhai Desai Road
Next to Talwalkars
Mumbai 400 036
MAP2 92

Nalli Sarees

Rs 200 - 45,000

As popular as the cuisine of the South, Nalli offers staple specialities to women. Although famous for its traditional silk brocades, the shop also keeps tanchois from Banaras, uppada kanjorams from Kanjipuram and casual cottons from Orissa. Embellished with embroidery, kundan, and zari work, the saris here are truly outstanding, and perfectly reflect the South's exquisite culture and flair.

DAILY 10-8

Shop No. 7
Tirupati Apartments
Bhulabhai Desai Road
Mumbai 400 026
Ph. 91 22 2496 5577/ 2496 5599, **MAP2 93**

Narendra Kumar

Rs 2,500 onwards

This former Elle editor made a niche in the fashion industry with his sharply tailored men's wear and his recent foray into Eve's land has been widely applauded as well. From lightly textured daywear mull shirts to structured fit jackets, the designer presents a pure western collection with innovative embroideries on body-conscious silhouettes. Patronized by the elegant Simi Garewal, Narendra Kumar's outfits are a cut above.

Unit 6, S.P. Centre
41/44 Minoo Desai Marg
Colaba,
Mumbai 400 005
Ph. 91 22 5638 5468

DAILY 10.30-7.30

Natalzee

Rs 500 - 4,000

A hot hello to the street-scorching and night-ranging chicks of Mumbai. Spice up your wardrobes with embroidered denims, sexy spaghettis and asymmetric skirts, designed to make you sizzle and shine. Then spruce up the look with quirky handbags, colourful beaded belts and evil eye bracelets, which sparkle out in the dark. Natalzee glistens from A to Zee.

Gr Floor, Vasundhara Building
5 Bhulabhai Desai Road
Mumbai 400 026
Ph. 91 22 2351 1367
MAP2 94

DAILY 11-7 (Sun closed)

Neeta Lulla

Prices on Request

Fashion goes fully filmi at Neeta Lulla's new store where you'll find your eyes wandering between star-studded ensembles and star patrons themselves! Heady colour combinations and eye-catching details define the prêt and diffusion numbers for men and women here, while bridal wear can be custom-ordered by appointment with the designer herself. So walk in here to buy yourself some glitter, glitz and glamour, with prices to match of course!

6 RNA Classic
SV Road
Santracruz (W)
Mumbai 400 054
Ph. 91 22 5576 5599
MAP1 95

www.neetalulla.com

DAILY 11-7.30 (Sun closed)

New Pink Lady

Rs 15 - 10,000

It's not the outfit that makes the lady, but the lady that makes the outfit. This Lady, however, tries to ensure, that she will have accessories to match any outfit you might choose. Offering acrylic, lac and crystal bangles with kundans and dangling jhumkas, the shop also has simply designed bindis and hair clips; all

136/ C
Sikka Nagar
V.P. Road
Mumbai 400 004
Ph. 91 22 2388 7370

accessorizing the blushed look with a pinky touch.

info@newpinklady.com
www.newpinklady.com

DAILY 10-9 (Sun closed)

Nike

Rs 250 - 6,000

Sport maniacs, this is your territory. Only the latest and lightest-weight sneakers climb up the racks here, while trademarked stay-dry tracks and jerseys sweat in style. The swoosh paraphernalia includes coordinated water sippers, signature caps, and sport bags, amongst the other ticked bits; giving all you speedies, everything you need to run the mile, spin the bike, or simply to sport the look.

DAILY 10.30-9

Parsi Agairy, 91 Janmabhumi Marg, Opp. Siddharth College, Dhobi Talao, Mumbai 400 008
Ph. 91 22 2207 6026

Jai Niketan, 16th Cross Road, Khar Danda Road
Khar (W), Mumbai 400 052, Ph. 91 22 2649 8470

570 Sarvananda Sadan, Opp. Laxmi Padam Maternity Hospital, 5th Road, Khar (W), Mumbai 400 052
Ph. 91 22 2604 8063

Skyzone, Phoenix Mills, Senapati Bapat Marg
Lower Parel, Mumbai 400 013
Ph. 91 22 2495 1797

6 Kings Building, Dr. Ambedkar Road
Opp. Parel Telephone Complex, Parel, Mumbai 400 012
Ph. 91 22 2410 3402

Nehru Road, Near Mehul Theatre, Above Mexx, Opp. Gala Nagar, Mulund (W), Mumbai 400 080
Ph. 91 22 2561 0893

Opp. Irla Nursing Home, Vile Parle (W)
Mumbai 400 056, Ph. 91 22 2671 5797, **MAP1 96**

Shop No. 3
Priyanka Co-op Housing Society
Opp. Atur Park
Sion - Tromboy Road
Chembur
Mumbai 400 071
Ph. 91 22 2520 1043

Shop No. 2
Shyam Vihar
Linking Road
Opp. Khar Telephone Exchange, Khar (W)
Mumbai 400 052
Ph. 91 22 2646 1696/ 2605 1269

14 Sun Swept Building, Lokhandwala Complex
Opp. Domino's, Andheri (W), Mumbai 400 053
Ph. 91 22 2633 1819

Tamarind
11/ B Cusrow Baug,
Shahid Bhagat Singh Rd
Colaba Causeway,
Mumbai 400 005
Ph. 91 22 2284 1821

Nimesis

Rs 550 - 1,050

Affordable style is the mantra here. On offer is a selection of club and casual wear and stylish accessories. Most of the goods in-store, are imported from the Far East, while the jeans are locally tailored. Between the run-of-the-mill products, the trendy sandals and handbags stand out, and could make a one-off buy.

nimesis_ext@rediffmail.com

DAILY 10.30-9.30

18, Amrapali Shopping Centre, Vile Parle,
Mumbai 400 056
Ph. 91 22 2614 1090

Nine West

Rs 1,700 - 8,000

This American import has gained quick popularity for fashionable leather shoes and accessories in India. Nine West offers everything from sandals and boots to practical chappals and sporty pumps. A selection of well-designed handbags is also available to match the colourful footwear.

Crossroads,
28, Pt. M.M. Malviya
Road, Haji Ali,
Mumbai 400 034

MON-FRI 10-9, SAT-SUN 10-9.30

Nisha Sagar

Rs 2,500 - 85,000

Popular with the who's who of Mumbai this couture mansion houses exquisite Indian creations. Specializing in handwork, the clothes speak of rich craftsmanship combined with delicate panache. Ideal for a bridal trousseau or even a glamorous evening party, the collections here include everything from semi-formal kurtis to heavy lehengas. Frothing with tinsel creations, this boutique has made a glittery niche for itself, especially amongst Bollywood's ritziest.

Kailash, 4th Road
Vallabh Nagar Society
J.V.P.D Scheme
Mumbai 400 056
MAP1 97

nishasagar@hotmail.com

DAILY 10-7 (Sun closed)

NU

Rs 250 - 3,500

Shoppers can easily accumulate a wardrobe of this store's hip products without even realizing it. Proudly proclaiming that it has every kind of western outfit from casual to office wear, NU has much on offer for women of all ages and budgets. With a focus on hand embroidery, the clothes stand out in their strategic cuts and attractive designs, while funky accessories match up in sprite.

New Poornima Apt.
23/2 Peddar Road
Near Jaslok Hospital
Mumbai 400 026
Ph. 91 22 2351 4846

DAILY 10.30-8 (Sun closed)

Offbeat

Rs 695 onwards

While taking the leap from onesome to twosome, try something a little offbeat. Specializing in groom's wear, this store has a range of heavy sherwanis and suits made of Italian fabrics, cotton weaves, and brocades. With most of the clothes in basic cuts and colours, the club wear shirts jazz up the ambience with abstract designs and contemporary fits.

5/ 6, Cornerview
15th & 33rd Road
Junction
Bandra (W)
Mumbai 400 050
Ph. 91 22 2600 6834/
5696 0460

TUE-SUN 11-9

Ofran

Rs 795 onwards

An offshoot of the famed Kachins Enterprise, Ofran stocks collections of casual and semi-formal clothes. Located in a separate area of the shop, business-wear shirts, blazers, and ties for men are higher in quality than the rest of the attires. Although bags, bracelets, and shoes for women decorate the shop's centre spot, the beaded stoles on the corner walls steal the limelight.

C 208-210
28, Pt. M.M. Malviya
Road, Crossroads
Haji Ali
Mumbai 400 034
Ph. 91 22 5660 3066/67

ofran@vsnl.com
www.kachins.com

DAILY 10-8.30

On My Own (OMO)

Rs 150 - 3,500

Earthy browns get a ray of hot sunshine at this warehouse-like store that is loaded with a mix of fun and folk. The kitschy garbs range from vibrant crushed skirts to white linen drawstring pants, while the kurtis, patialas and dupattas infuse a touch of tradition to the entire range. Funky jewellery, shelled belts and patchwork bags complete the indo-chic look and like everything else here, can be bought 'on their own'.

204, 2nd Fl. Sagar
Fortune
Waterfield Road
Bandra (W)
Mumbai 400 050
Ph. 91 22 56981804
MAP1 98

arti2@rediffmail.com

DAILY 11-7.30 (Sun closed)

Only Woman

Rs 59 - 1,020

Women can buy their privacy at this store which sells only lingerie. Bras, panties, and camisoles in basic colours can be found here, along with daily wear undergarment sets in pastels. The merchandise at the shop comes from standard labels such as Lovable and Vanity Fair, while all the products are available from beginners to plus sizes.

R - Mall, L.B.S Marg
Mulund (W)
Mumbai 400 080
Ph. 91 22 5643 0616

lovable@bgl.vsnl.net.in

DAILY 11.30-8.30

Oobç

Rs 299 - 1,200

Originally a ladies-wear store, Oobç has recently started a small line of clothing for men. Most popular for its casual tops, the shop's selection ranges from party wear clothes and gym gear, to business-casual

Shop No. 5
Phoenix Mills
462, Senapati Bapat
Marg, Lower Parel (W)
Mumbai 400 013
Ph. 91 22 5660 2932

attire. The clothes here are plain and uncomplicated; most suitable for those who prefer blending in rather than making heads turn.

DAILY 10.30-9.30

Shop No. L 4, Ground Floor,
InOrbit Mall, Mind Space
Link Road, Malad (W), Mumbai 400 064
Ph. 91 22 5643 0306

Shop No. 19
Sunny Side Cooperative
Housing Society
Lokhandwala Market
Andheri (W)
Mumbai 400 058
Ph. 91 22 5697 5460

Shop No. S 17
Centre 1 Shopping Mall
Sector 30 A, Vashi
Mumbai 400 703
Ph. 91 22 2781 2026

Open Secrets & Lifestyles

Rs 375 onwards

This store presents a small selection of Victoria's Secret lingerie, overshadowed by a plethora of exciting Bath & Body Works toiletries. Basic designs in cotton briefs include G-strings, thongs, bikini-styles and high-legs, all high in quality, but minimal in choice.

C206 Crossroads,
28, Pt. M.M. Malviya Rd.
Haji Ali,
Mumbai 400 034
Ph. 91 22 5660 2114

osls@satyam.net.in

DAILY 10.30-8.30 (Sun closed)

Orange Plum

Rs 975 onwards

A mixed basket of Indian and western products, this store cuts its clothes in refreshing designs with fruity colours Oozing the colour orange, with a tang of plum, the shop's belle patrons can dance in polka-dotted sarongs, while their awestruck cadits can laze in breezy cottons. A range of saris and kurtis add to the shop's dreamy collections; while the warm glow from within allures customers in.

Maskati Corner
G - 2, Ground Floor
Altamount Road
Mumbai 400 036
Ph. 91 22 3951 2369/
2381 3979

shop@orange-plum.com

DAILY 10-7 (Sun closed)

Originals Unlimited!

Rs 155 - 999

This family store claims to have original clothing from international brands like Gap and Old Navy. Men and women can find a variety of western clothes and daily wear shoes here, while the Toy Kingdom on the upper level cheers clothes in happy hues for tiny tots. A reasonable store with average quality clothing, you will find variety unlimited here!

Dhun - Abad
106, Bhulabhai Desai Rd
Junction of Warden
Road & Napean Sea
Road
Mumbai 400 036
Ph. 91 22 2369 5306/
2369 0557

erach@vsnl.com

DAILY 10-8.30

Oz

Rs 450 - 5,000

Soak yourself into the fashion world with this anorexic looking, thin and long shop. With slim fits and daring cuts, the clothes here range from sequins-studded tops and racer backs to crushed skirts and fad jeans. The bags and shoes deserve a second look as well, while the men's collection of club wear match-up in spirit.

DAILY 11-9

Shop No. 6
Jewel Arcade
Water Field Road
Opp A.K. Motiwala
Bandra (W)
Mumbai 400 050
Ph. 91 22 5625 0977

Paaneri

Rs 99 onwards

The collections at Paaneri are so remarkable that the mannequins come alive in them, à la their TV advertisements. A shop that has Indian clothes for women of all ages, Paaneri has saris and salwar kameezes, laboured with embroidery work. Specializing in double paloo, sarong and dhoti drapes, this store has something for every femme.

DAILY 9-9

217 Ceasars Court
Housing Society
S.V. Road, Andheri (W)
Mumbai 400 058
Ph. 91 22 2628 3738/
2628 8692, **MAP1 99**

372 Dadarkar Building
N.C. Kelkar Road
Dadar (W)
Mumbai 400 028
Ph. 91 22 2437 9934/35

Pagli

Rs 100-50,000

Continuing on from where its name left off, Pagli has 'crazy' varieties of Indian and western clothes. Trendy new designs accompany the store's clothing (both casual and formal), while lingerie and footwear fulfil basic needs. Boasting of decent quality products at conservative prices, this mad-hatters-clothes-party offers its local customers a handy shopping retreat.

pagli@vsnl.com; www.pagli.com

MON-WED 10-9.30, FRI-SUN 10-9.30

38, Citi Centre, S.V.
Road, Goregaon (W)
Mumbai 400 062
Ph. 91 22 2876 2828/
2877 2828

Palate

Rs 200 onwards

Created by Malini Akerkar, Ali Mamaji and Anuradha Singhania, Palate is a lavishly sprawled 6000 square-feet home fashion store. Art meets style here as exclusive fabrics for home furnishings, imported South-east Asian furniture and artifacts, along with some outdoor furniture are displayed here. Also offering personalised interior and styling services for homes and institutions, Palate promises to furnish your home with some delectable items.

DAILY 10-8

Badamia Manor
Clerk 34 Road
(lane next to ICICI Bank)
Off Racecourse
Mahalaxmi
Mumbai 400 011
Ph. 91 22 2498 3575

Pantaloons

Rs 50 onwards

'India's family store', Pantaloons is a trendy choice in self-service shopping accompanied with a friendly ambience. Offering competent clothing with frilly accessories, this departmental store serves all age ranks. With high quality products at even better prices; make sure you head to this plaza for a truly sumptuous experience.

sanjay.katara@ho.pantaloon.com
www.pantaloon.com

MON-FRI 11-9, SAT-SUN 11-9.30

Crossroads, 28 Pt. M.M. Malviya Road
Haji Ali, Mumbai 400 026

Phoenix Mills
462 Senapati Bapat Marg
Lower Parel
Mumbai 400 013
Ph. 91 22 5666 4848

Centre 1, Sector 30 A,
Vashi, Mumbai 400 703
Ph. 91 22 2781 2616

Paradise Tower, Thane,
Mumbai 400 601

✱ Paraphernalia

Rs 4,000 onwards

Chic, elegant and succulent are some of the words that come to mind when one thinks of designers Pallavi and Bhairavi Jaikishen. Translucent chiffons, bright floral embroidery and old brocades flavour Pallavi's saris, while daughter Bhairavi makes music with romantic drapes and art-deco motifs. The zesty indo-western prêt lines and glamorous bridal collections are 'must haves' in every trousseau treasury, while the indulgence can be completed with handmade 'Napoleon' chocolates. They just melt...

DAILY 10.30-7 (Sun closed)

Pagar Apt,
Peddar Road,
Mumbai 400 00
Ph. 91 22 2351 1987
MAP2 100

Valencia Building,
Juhu Tara Road,
Mumbai 400 049
Ph. 91 22 5679 7480

Part 1 Accessories

Rs 395 - 3,000

The younger sister to Habit Shoes, Part 1 Accessories has everything offered by its sibling, and more. A distributor for international brands such as Lee Cooper, Oakleys, and Adidas, this trading post, matches up to its style-savvy neighbours, with high-quality products at discounted prices.

DAILY 11-9 (Sun closed)

Shop No. 5
Candy Plaza
Rahin Mansion No. 2
Colaba Causeway
Mumbai 400 039
Ph. 91 22 2202 0864

Passion Flower

Rs 450 - 3,000

One of the only shops offering trousseau nightwear and lingerie, Passion Flower instantly gains a slot for itself. Sheer lacy baby-doll sets are completed with bras, thongs and gowns for champagne-and-strawberry nights, while the hotter varieties include tiger-print

Shop No R-1, Linking Road Extension,
Near Juhu Lions Garden,
Santacruz (W),
Mumbai 400 054
Ph. 91 22 2660 5927
MAP1 101

halter-neck tops and tiny boxers in satin. On the comfort zone, the kaftans and daily-wear kurtis make for appropriate bedroom lounging.

DAILY 11-7 (Sun closed)

Payal Singhal

Rs 5,000 onwards

Offering a niche indo-western line for the younger generation, Payal Singhal's ensembles personify fusion haute couture. Signature beaded stoles and tassels dress up spicy colours in daring silhouette, where western styling along with heavy traditional embellishments present a unique collection of bridal lehengas. Lavishly à la mode with price tags to match, this shop manages to steal the hearts of many a ravishing beauties.

www.payalsinghal.com

DAILY 10.30-7.30 (Sun closed)

Shop No.1, Fiona Building,
Juhu Tara Road,
Mumbai 400 054
Ph. 91 22 2660 9810

Shop No.4, Raj Mahal,
33 Altamount Road,
Mumbai 400 026
Ph. 91 22 2386 9139
MAP2 102

✷ Peacock Forever

Rs 1,900 - 9,000

A popular haunt with Bollywood's glitziest; Falguni & Shane offer style like nobody else. Inimitable poncho tops made of pashmina shawls, and denim jackets with brocade trims dress up winter blues; while cool chiffons with one-off motifs and mull kurtis with stones, aglow sun-kissed days. Playing peek-a-boo with various fabric mediums, each garment at the shop defines its own style.

www.peacockcouture.com

DAILY 10.30-7.30 (Sun closed)

Shop No. 1
Hanvant Bhavan
80-E Napean Sea Road
Mumbai 400 036
Ph. 91 22 2367 4531
MAP1 103

Pepe

Rs 349 onwards

Slim at the waist, generous at the thighs and tapering downwards, the jeans at Pepe work like magic for girls. A playful selection of tops for regular and sportswear is fizzed up with a dash of energetic colours and relaxed fits here. Most famous for its 'fashion jeans', Pepe provides products that can last a lifetime; after all, good jeans never die, they just fade away...

DAILY 11-8.30 (Sun closed)

27 Raghuvanshi Estate, Senapati Bapat Marg, L. Parel,
Mumbai 400 013
Ph. 91 22 2498 5021/ 2491 0236

Heera Panna Shopping Centre, Haji Ali, Mumbai 400 026
Ph. 91 22 2498 3081

14-A Cusrow Baug
Colaba Causeway
Mumbai 400 005
Ph. 91 22 2283 2161

346 Saffron Building
Linking Road
Bandra (W)
Mumbai 400 050
Ph. 91 22 2605 9155/
2605 0996

Peppertree

Rs 40 - 1,200

Cheap meets hip at this little booth that stacks everything from crushed skirts and backless cholis to wooden jewellery and silver anklets. Specializing in fusion designs, the store satiates the dressing needs of all those craving the Kareena Kapoor gypsy-look in 'Yuva'. Don't rely on the quality of the products though; the clothes will have a short life span.

DAILY 11-8 (Sun closed), (Tardeo)
DAILY 12-9.30 (Andheri)

Shop No. 3
Vaidya Mansion
Opp Crossroads, Tardeo
Mumbai 400 007
Ph. 91 22 2494 1905

52 RNA Shopping
Arcade
Lokhandwala Complex
Andheri (W)
Mumbai 400 053
Ph. 91 22 2630 4259

Phat Fish

Rs 500 onwards

This fish makes the crossover from cool to chic. The hot and tempting numbers here promise to reinvent your wardrobe whether you're looking for casual tees, a sexy skirt or stringy bikinis. Boys can bubble in too for a cool collection of club and casual wear; other baits include an enticing range of belts, footwear and trinkets.

DAILY 11.30-8.30

Hira Villa Apartments
3 Pali Hill Road
Opp HSBC Bank
Bandra (W)
Mumbai 400 050
Ph. 91 22 2640 7893

Pinakin

Prices On Request

If you're conjuring up relaxed images of Alibagh beach houses, wooden furniture and collectible pottery, you're bang on! Pinakin Patel's flagship furniture store has stuff that'll fit stylishly into every home, traditional or contemporary. Celebrating wood in deep brown chests, rosewood tables, craggy floor pieces, or even as background for ivory-coloured carved Buddhas and ancient Indian sculptures, each item here is a novelty by itself – with prices to match.

DAILY 10-8 (Sun closed)

Raghuvanshi Mills
Compound
Senapati Bapat Marg
Lower Parel
Mumbai 400 013
Ph. 91 22 5600 2500
MAP2 104

Piramyd

Rs 150-6,000

Loaded with clothing, accessories, cosmetics and home-ware, this store provides an inspiring environment for family shopping. Overflowing with Indian and international brands, the shop offers some great bargains; while the ladies indo-western mix-n-match section makes self custom-designing fun and easy.

DAILY 10-9

Crossroads
28, Pt. M.M. Malviya Rd
Haji Ali
Mumbai 400 034
Ph. 91 22 2494 5890

Pitambari

Rs 700 - 8,000

A Kolkata based brand, Pitambari is especially known for its hand and machine embroidered saris. Although most popular for its georgettes and crepes, the store also keeps block prints and bandhanis. Apart from the ready-made collections available here, custom-made orders for saris are accepted as well.

DAILY 10.30-7 (Sun closed)

22 Bhulabhai Desai Rd
Mahalaxmi Chambers
Mumbai 400 026
Ph. 91 22 2351 9787

Plot No. 9
Gurmohar Road No. 1
J.V.P.D Scheme
Mumbai 400 049
Ph. 91 22 3095 7246
MAP2 105

Planet Fashion

Rs 250 onwards

Replenishing your power-dressing wardrobe, Planet Fashion offers a comprehensive range of men's wear. Spiffy suits, shirts and trousers come from the houses of Allen Solly, Van Huesen and Louise Philippe, while the casual wear sections include 'clean jeans' and hassle-free t-shirts.

DAILY 11-9

Crossroads
28, Pt. M.M. Malviya Rd
Haji Ali
Mumbai 400 034
Ph. 91 22 2200 6242

8 Tirupati Apts
Opp. Mahalaxmi Temple
Mumbai 400 034
Ph. 91 22 2491 4611
MAP2 106

Planet Sports

Rs 89 - 10,000

A full-field store for the diehard sports fans, Planet Sports keeps internationally branded clothing and accessories. Sporting everything from swimsuits to tracks, this store is a one-stop shop away from looking and feeling fit. Catering to all, but especially to college students, 'as they are more fit conscious'; it is about time you 'ever-green at heart' ones start giving the younger lot, a run for their money.

crp@planetsportsindia.com

DAILY 11-9

4th Floor
Piramyd Megastore
Crossroads
28 Pt. M.M. Malviya
Road, Haji Ali
Mumbai 400 034
Ph. 91 22 5662 7099

Shop No. 3
Abhindan Housing
Society
Dr. Ambedkar Road
Next to Premier Cinema
Lower Parel
Mumbai 400 013
Ph. 91 22 2415 0379

Potion 9

Rs 375 - 2,000

A style tonic for the fashion-struck, men and women will be remedied here. Ingredients imported straight from the Far East include club wear, funky earrings and trendy belts with a dash of local denims. Sequinned totes and flip-flops with kitten heels add their scores here, while men's curly-toe leather shoes spice up the potion with some Indian masala.

DAILY 10.30-8.30
SUN 4.30-8.30

2, Orten's Enterprises,
Opp. Amarsons,
Bandra (W),
Mumbai 400 050
Ph. 91 22 2644 2759

Pramanik

Rs 100 - 9,000

A collage of colours greet you at this store. The shararas, tops, and indo-western outfits keep the women busy, while men entertain themselves with casual and business clothing to furnish their wardrobes. Sherwanis and kurta pyjamas stand smartly in their places, while clothing and accessories for kids spoil the little ones with variety.

enquiry@pramanikindia.com
www.pramanikindia.com

TUE-SUN 9.30-8.30

360 K.N. Building
Bhandarkar Road
Matunga (C.R.)
Mumbai 400 019
Ph. 91 22 2410 5112
MAP2 107

Pratap

Prices on Request

Rajesh Pratap Singh's clothes are famous for their fit, finish and understated, yet keen design detail. Mostly found in basic and earthy colours, the structured suits and sherwanis for men exude finesse and class, while the range of chromatic crushed skirts aglow the sandy racks. Leather sandals with quilted soles add to the shop's international flavour; while also matching up to the rest of the products in comfort and excellence.

DAILY 11-7.30

C - 202
Crossroads
28, Pt. M.M. Malviya Rd
Haji Ali
Mumbai 400 034

The Courtyard
S.P. Centre
41/ 44 Minoo Desai
Marg, Colaba
Mumbai 400 005

Pretty walk

Rs 180 - 3,000

Prettify your peds with shoes from this store that offers dainty products of casual lace ups and diamante studded kitten heels. Shoes from international brands such as Fila, Lee Cooper and Red Tape make an entry here, while macho men can also find some pretty peddings for themselves.

DAILY 11-9.30 (Sun closed)

R Mall, Level Two
Shop No. 10/ 11
L.B.S Marg, Mulund (W)
Mumbai 400 080
Ph. 91 22 5598 2774

73, Galleria
Hiranandani Garden
Powai, Mumbai 400 076
Ph. 91 22 2579 7740/
2579 7032

Private Collections

Prices on Request

Remixing the era of the sultans with the aura of today's youth, this store offers collections for trend-conscious divas. Silhouettes dripping in diamantes look gorgeous on lehengas with racer back cholis, and kurtas with asymmetrical dupattas. To attract some private attention on occasions that truly matter; all you powder-puffed girlies, make sure you prance through this shop's collections.

zeenat@privatecollectionsindia.com

DAILY 11-7 (Sun closed)

14, Vasundhara
Mahalaxmi
Mumbai 400 026
Ph. 91 22 2352 1840/41
MAP2 108

Priya & Chintan

Rs 5,000 - 80,000

Promising debutants from the 'Femina Young Designers Award-2004', Priya & Chintan showcase in their collections, a fusion of ethnic elements from around the world. Rustic colours and embellishments are stylized in western forms to give the clothes a traditional yet contemporary look. Conversely, their prêt collection includes bold corsets, slinky skirts and tapering jute pants, for all those who dare to bare.

www.priyaandchintan.com

DAILY 11-8 (Sun closed) Appt preferred

49 Prem Court,
Peddar Road,
Mumbai 400 026
Ph. 91 98210 46644
Mob. 91 98216 27261

Provogue

Rs 895-1,395

Ideal for afternoon lounging, Provogue's range of striped, textured and monotoned shirts in peachy colours are cosy and comfortable. On a more serious note, the brand also has polysonic business and formal shirts and t-shirts, along with cotton pants and ties, to make a breezy and unruffled impression in the corporate sphere.

www.provogue.net

DAILY 11-9

Sports Telecom, Shop No. 10, Sion Trombay Road
Opp. Diamond Garden, Chembur (E), Mumbai 400 071
Ph. 91 22 5599 3799/ 2869 3892, **MAP1 108**

104, Heera Panna, Haji Ali, Mumbai 400 026
Ph. 91 22 2351 2498

Crossroads
28, Pt. M.M. Malviya Rd
Haji Ali
Mumbai 400 034
Ph. 91 22 5660 7185

Shop No. 15
Sunny Site
Co-op Housing Society
Lokhandwala Complex
Andheri (W)
Mumbai 400 053
Ph. 91 22 2631 7802/
2869 3892

Khan Manzil
Linking Road
Bandra (W)
Mumbai 400 059
Ph. 91 22 5693 1846/
2869 3893

Provogue Lounge

Rs 245 - 2,500

This brand believes in selling a lifestyle, not just a product. So, as the sun shines, clothes with psychedelic designs and short colours sheen the more exciting end, while cotton kurtis, striped knits and trousers dress up functional wear. But as darkness falls, the shelves, and in fact the entire store simply camouflages into a nightclub; enticing customers to rock and roll.

DAILY 11-9.30

Phoenix Mills,
462 Senapati Bapat
Marg,
Lower Parel,
Mumbai 400 013
Ph. 91 22 2497 2525

Puravi Modgil

Rs 1,000 onwards

For a designer outfit at dress-down prices, Puravi Modgil is a fine option. Concentrating on detailing and embroidery, the designer's forte lies in her heavily embellished saris. Kurtis, salwar kameezes and lehengas in rejuvenating colours can also be bought here; all promising to add spirit and sprite to any special occasion.

puravimodgil@hotmail.com

DAILY 11-6 (Sun closed)

20 Udadhi Tarang
Society, Next to J. W
Marriot Hotel, Juhu Rd
Mumbai 400 049
Ph. 91 98210 36975
MAP1 110

Purple Kids

Rs 120 - 800

This new-kid-on-the-block is a brand 'only for energetic little boys with attitude'. A value-for-money option, this store for boys combines comfort with style. Energy levels soar high here, with miniature sky-blue Indian cricket-team t-shirts cheering for sale, while the cartoon-prints tees are especially cute, in reds, blues and purple.

DAILY 10-9

1st Road, Near Orange Shop, Chembur
Mumbai 400 071, Ph. 91 22 2528 5560

Discount Store, Near S.K. Dairy, Virar (W)
Mumbai 401 303, Ph. 91 22 5597 4278

Flat No.11, Ground Floor
Harichand Textile Mill Compound
Vikhroli, Mumbai 400 079, Ph. 91 22 2539 9230

Centre One
Vashi
Mumbai 4000 703
Ph. 91 22 2781 2370

R-Mall
Mulund (W)
Mumbai 400 080
Ph. 91 22 2592 4233

Ram Maruti Road
Thane-Lokhandwala
Complex
Andheri (W)
Mumbai 400 053
Ph. 91 22 2635 0337

Mongibai Road
Vile Parle (E)
Mumbai 400 057
Ph. 91 22 2613 0746

 Q!

Rs 100 onwards

Razzle and dazzle with this undiscovered gem of a shop at the muddled Maker Arcade. J-Lo pants with a string of horizontal belts, quilted short skirts dipped in glitter, and embroidered denims, are speckled around the shop; while oomphy slim-fit dresses and noodle tops neatly line against the walls. Q-ing up on the accessories racks are golden belts, bright fashion sneakers and butterfly studded slip-ons; all vivacious, fun and a little naughty. Just like the shop, you'll glow girl!

meghanasood@hotmail.com

DAILY 10.30-8.30 (Sun closed)

74 Maker Arcade
Cuffe Parade
Mumbai 400 005
Ph. 91 22 3092 2774
MAP2 111

Queens Emporium

Rs 500 - 1,00,000

If the plethora of sari shops in Marine Lines has not depleted your will to shop, walk in here to discover some silken dreams. Specializing in interwoven silks, Queens Emporium presents an exquisite collection of Banarsis and South Indian saris. Expect to be looking at the 'most

89 Queen's Chambers,
MK Marg,
Marine Lines,
Mumbai 400 020
Ph. 91 22 2206 3805

exclusive designs' from enthusiastic sales staff trying to charm you with their keen sales pitches.

queens@vsnl.com
www.queenssilks.com

DAILY 11-7 (Sun closed)

Rabani & Rakha

Rs 19,500 onwards

Bursting with colour and opulence, the Indian clothes at Rabani & Rakha boast of rich craftsmanship and admirable elegance. Although popular for their resham, mukaish and kundan work, the designers also use crystal and mirror embellishments to prettify their plush outfits. Teamed with halters and spaghetti tops, their saris are ideal for women who mix femininity with flair. Pretty, perky and ultra glam, say hello to the new fashion queen within you!

Store No 9
The Courtyard
41/ 44 Minoo Desai
Marg, Colaba
Mumbai 400 005
Ph. 91 22 5638 5476/77

rrabani@hotmail.com

DAILY 10.30-7.30

Radhika Naik

Rs 30,000 onwards

Operating by appointment only, Radhika Naik makes 'one time' traditional outfits. Embellished with sequins and coloured crystals, her clothes have vibrant combinations and exquisite designs. Outfits that exude sophistication and class, coupled with personalized attention from the designer; it's no wonder that the la-di-da ladies of Mumbai give this little shop a big thumbs-up.

No. 6 Sea View Terrace
68-71 Wodehouse Road
Colaba
Mumbai 400 005
Ph. 91 22 2216 1433/34
MAP2 112

radhika_naik@vsnl.net

BY APPOINTMENT ONLY

Ragz Genes

Rs 695 - 1,395

A disappointment for all you aspiring rock stars and a pleasant surprise for all their mothers; this tiny red shop offers a variety of 'decent' trousers, cargos, and three-fourths. No discriminations here, the clothes are unisex, except for a small range of shirts exclusively for men. Concentrating on three kinds of trouser fits: boot cuts, anti-fits and regulars; this shop offers reasonable quality products at civilized prices.

248 Linking Road
Opp. National College
Bandra (W)
Mumbai 400 050
Ph. 91 22 2642 1127/
2640 9063

DAILY 10-9

Rahul Agasti

Rs 2,000 - 8,000

An all-male store, Rahul Agasti has supreme quality clothing for casual, formal and groom's wear. Most popular for its custom-made attires, the shop also offers handmade suits, two layered sherwanis and bold monotoned shirts. Catering to Mumbai's tinsel-towners, the clothes here boast of style and finesse, while the small range of ties and belts complete the classy act. Women look out – Rahul Agasti will soon be out to dress you too.

rahul_agasti@hotmail.com

DAILY 11-8.30 (Sun closed)

Aryston Centre
Opp. J.W. Marriot Hotel
Juhu, Mumbai 400 049
Ph. 91 22 2615 3988
MAP1 113

Rainbow

Rs 500 onwards

Nothing chromatic about this store, Rainbow has casual and semi-formal clothes in sober colours for men. Made with imported fabrics the knitted shirts and linen trousers make comfortable and good looking lounge wear, while jeans from Levi's, Pepe and Spykar add to the relaxed look and feel of the shop.

TUE-SUN 11.30-10.30

74/ 75 Citi Mall
Fame Ad Labs, New Link Road, Andheri (W)
Mumbai 400 053
Ph. 91 22 5698 2546

4 Indraprasth Shopping Centre,
S.V. Road, Borivali (W)
Mumbai 400 092
Ph. 91 22 2863 0181

Raj Kamal Sarees

Rs 2,000 onwards

A specialist in lehengas, Raj Kamal Sarees has clothes loaded with stone and resham work. Bursting with energetic colours, the shop also displays a range of kurtis and saris. For a rich and extravagant look with unexaggerated prices, this store can strew a lady's path with compliments and flowers galore.

DAILY 10-6 (Sun closed)

384-A
Dabholkar Wadi
1st Floor
Kalbadevi Road
Mumbai 400 002
Ph. 91 22 2201 0047/ 2208 9711

Rangoli

Rs 250 - 10,000

Synonomous with its name, Rangoli is a spectrum of colours with various types of saris dangling from its racks. Ranging from traditional paithanis sets to ghadwals from Andhra Pradesh, this store scouts various collections of casual and bridal wear. Most famous for their embroidery work, the products here will add splashes of lively hues to your closet.

TUE-SUN 9.30-8.30

5 Laxmi Building
N.C. Kelkar Road
Dadar, Mumbai 400 028
Ph. 91 22 2436 1099/ 2422 1499

372 Dadarkar Building
N.C. Kelkar Road
Dadar (W)
Mumbai 400 028
Ph. 91 22 2430 8009

Rasulbhai Adamji

Rs 350 - 3,000

A familiar name, Rasulbhai Adamji is a modest retail store that has maintained its reputation in supreme-quality leather accessories, for many decades. The European influenced handbags exhibit a dramatic range in styles, from classics to college funk. Other accessories here, include belts, office sets, portfolios, and travel bags.

rasulbhaiadamji@vsnl.com
www.rasulbhaiadamji.com

DAILY 11-7 (Sun closed)

48, Colaba Causeway,
Next to Colaba Police Station,
Mumbai 400 001
Ph. 91 22 2202 6097 / 1267, **MAP2 114**

Ravissant

Rs 3,000 onwards

Prance into a world seething opulence and find all that is desired to live a princely lifestyle. The range is from saris, salwar kameezes and indo-westerns, to cocktail ensembles, trousseau and bridal wear. Kurta pyjamas and shirts for men spell luxury, while a lavish line of silverware and jewellery rise up to the shop's high standards. This boutique is a wonderland in disguise, so leave your guilt behind and indulge.

DAILY 9.30-8 (Sun closed)

17 A Cooperage Road, New India Centre Building,
Mumbai 400 039, Ph. 91 22 2287 3405/06

131, August Kranti Marg,
Kemps Corner,
Mumbai 400 026
Ph. 91 22 2363 7003/ 2368 4934, **MAP2 115**

Oberoi Towers,
L/14 Lobby Level,
Marine Drive,
Mumbai 400 020
Ph. 91 22 2284 2586

The Taj Mahal Hotel
Apollo Bunder
Mumbai 400 001
Ph. 91 22 2281 5227

Raymond's

Rs 795 - 2,000

Shine the spotlight on your business wear with clothing from Raymond's. Available here are a collection of formal shirts and trousers from Park Avenue, a business-casual range from Parx and casual lounge attire from Color Plus. Classically designed in stark colours, Raymond's provides a 'complete look for the complete man'.

Central Avenue Road,
Near Ambedkar Garden,
Chembur, Mumbai 400 071
Ph. 91 22 2558 1922
Daily 10.30-8 (Mon closed)

237 J.N. Road, Mulund (W)
Mumbai 400 080
Ph. 91 22 2569 0421
Daily 10.30-8 (Thurs closed)

R Mall, Shop No. 1A & 1B 639, L.B.S. Marg, Mulund,
Mumbai 400 080, Ph. 91 22 5555 0813

Mid Town, S.V. Road, Borivali, Mumbai 400 092
Ph. 91 22 2862 8650
Daily 10.30-8 (Thurs closed)

59-A
Bhulabhai Desai Road
Mumbai 400 026
wdrd47006@vsnl.net
Daily 10.30 - 8

RNA House Veer
Nariman Road
Mumbai 400 001
Ph. 91 22 2204 5912
Daily 10.30 - 8 (Sun closed)

Moneera Lodge
20 Colaba Causeway
Mumbai 400 001
Ph. 91 22 22020434
MAP2 116
Daily 10.30 - 8 (Sun closed)

5/6 Sompuri
Market Station Road
Santacruz (W)
Mumbai 400 054
Ph. 91 22 2649 0428
Daily 10.30 - 8

62 World Trade Centre, Cuffe Parade, Colaba, Mumbai 400 005, Ph. 91 22 2218 1423
Daily 10.30- 8 (Sun closed)

Arvind Niwas Sandhurst Bridge, Opera House, Mumbai 400 007
Ph. 91 22 2369 0049
Daily 10.30- 8

88 Empire Mahal, 806 Dr. Ambedkar Road Mumbai 400 014, Ph. 91 22 2412 4425
Daily 10.30- 8

New Hind House, N.M. Marg, Ballard Estate, Mumbai 400 038, Ph. 91 22 2261 8321
Daily 10.30-8 (Sun closed)

109/110
Malad Shopping Centre
S.V. Road
Malad (W)
Mumbai 400 064
Ph. 91 22 2889 1195
Daily 10.30 - 8 (Thurs closed)

Red Blue & Yellow

Rs 3,000 onwards

From basic to exotic, this palette captures every hue of comfort in its affordable range of furniture and home accessories. From chaise-lounges and reclining sofas to cabinets and dining tables, all the furniture here comes in various shapes and sizes. The furnishing textures here range from plush leather to earthy jute, ensuring that you find just the right blend to create your look.

DAILY 11-8 (Sun closed)

G11 Laxmi Estate
Shakti Mill Lane
Mahalaxmi
Mumbai 400 011
Ph. 91 22 5666 2641

President House
Colaba
Mumbai 400 005
Ph. 91 22 2218 7739
MAP2 117

Reebok

Rs 99 - 6,990

As the old saying goes, runners never die, only their soles do. You definitely won't have that problem with this brand's high-quality shoes. Reebok has a range of sports attires, a casual line from Rockport, and a classy golf collection from Greg Norman. A reputed name with durable products, this chain has a homogeneous mix of fun, funk and flair.

DAILY 10.30-9.30

'Dawn' Plot No. 328
Corner of 7th Rad & Linking Road, Khar (W)
Mumbai 400 052
Ph. 91 22 2649 8315/ 2649 8311

5 Chaitania Co-op Housing Society
Tejpal Scheme Road # 2
Vile Parle (E)
Mumbai 400 057
Ph. 91 22 2682 6745/ 2836 3813

Regal Shoes

Rs 295 - 10,000

Although capturing a pretty range of shoes for women, Regal's forte lies in its men's leather footwear. Charming kids with its small stompers, this shop also stocks international brands like Lee Cooper and Red Tape. Beaded handbags join the parade of products, while everything here tags level-headed prices.

DAILY 10-10

Holiday Inn, Juhu, Mumbai 400 049
Ph. 91 22 5693 4356

5 Dharam Palace
Hughes Road
Mumbai 400 007
Ph. 91 22 2369 3876

Oberoi Towers
Nariman Point
Mumbai 400 021
Ph. 91 22 2287 0839

InOrbit Mall
Linking Road
Malad
Mumbai 400 064
Ph. 91 22 2876 1786

Reia

Prices on Request

This shop stocks a range of jadao sets, payals, maangtikas and jhumkas for ethnic beauties, while contemporary watches and pendants attract the less conventional types. The 1 gram gold sets, bangles and rings available here come in handy for gifting or personal wear, especially if one has a budget in mind.

DAILY 11.30-9

Shop No.8,
Patel Shopping Centre,
Chandavarkar Lane,
Borivali (W),
Mumbai 400 0092
Ph. 91 22 2864 9617

R Mall, LBS Marg,
Mulund (W),
Mumbai 400 080
Ph. 91 22 5555 0773

Reid & Taylor

Rs 745 - 10,000

When Amitabh Bachchan endorses a brand of clothing, it is bound to be of supreme quality. Internationally renowned, Reid & Taylor makes everything from linen pin-tucks, and striped shirts, to jazzy club wear tops. Suits in shades of blacks, greys and blues are available here as well, while orders for tail coats and tuxedos are readily accepted. Truly, you can't go wrong, when you 'bond with the best'.

DAILY 10.30-8.30

Mohammed Haji Adam & Co., 84 Sheriff Devji Street,
Masjid, Mumbai 400 003
Ph. 91 22 2342 3166/ 2345 1011

55 - A V.N. Road
Flora Fountain
Mumbai 400 023
Ph. 91 22 2204 2630

Bhagwan Collections
Santacruz (W)
Mumbai 400 054
Ph. 91 22 2649 3468/
2649 1601

Remanika

Rs 400 - 3,500

A seriously with-it shop, Remanika brings hip and faddy products to the masses. With colours from across the spectrum, the clothes are embellished with sequins and satin trims. The asymmetrical skirts, printed pants and polka-dotted shirts are especially eye-catching, while the jewellery, belts and bags are straight out of a fashion magazine. So all you girls with ten-on-ten bodies, spin in to catch the rage!

www.remanika.com

DAILY 9.30-9.30

Shop No. A-5, Ground Floor, Crystal Plaza
Link Road, Andheri (W), Mumbai 400 056
Ph. 91 22 2674 2260

162 Chinoy Mansion
1st floor, Warden Road
Mumbai 400 036
Ph. 91 22 2364 0860
MAP2 **118**

'R' Mall
L.B.S. Marg, Mulund (W)
Mumbai 400 080
Ph. 91 22 5599 3524

At Pantaloon
Phoenix Mills
462, Senapati Bapat
Marg
Lower Parel
Mumbai 400 013
Ph. 91 22 5666 4825

Reshma

Rs 4,000 onwards

A small boutique strewn with beach stones, Reshma offers clothes ranging from indo-western kurtis to bridal lehengas. Concentrating on embroidery, the designer prides herself in superior quality clothing

Navjivan Building
Shop No. 1
20 Napean Sea Road
Mumbai 400 036
Ph. 91 22 2369 3060

and fine workmanship. For a last-minute special occasion buy, keep this fashion nook in mind.

DAILY 10.30-7.30 (Sun closed)

151 Ghadiyal Gali
Mangaldas Market
Mumbai 400 002
Ph. 91 22 2206 9108

Revolution

Rs 299 - 1,499

Break the size barrier...it's time for a Revolution! Catering to women with fuller silhouettes, this shop racks simple yet stylish clothing. From casual trousers and capris to formal shell tops and crushed skirts, the garbs here are cheery in cuts and fits. Most popular on board are the tummy tucking 'magic trousers' that are purposefully designed to camouflage those extra inches.

customercare@revolution.bz

DAILY 11-8.30 (Sun closed)

6 Jains Arcade
14th Cross
Off Linking Road
Khar (W)
Mumbai 400 052
Ph. 91 22 2605 8483/
3096 1335, MAP1 119

1st Plot
Bhulabhai Desai Road
Next to Crossword Book Stall
Mumbai 400 026
Ph. 91 22 2492 1181

✱ Revolutions

Rs 125 - 2,500

Providing a breakthrough in shoe shopping, this urbane construction successfully lives up to its name. Resting besides trendy casual-bags, the transparent Cinderella sandals and nattily netted clogs bag all the prizes, while sneakers strive to sneak their way up. Lauding a large range of men's classic shoes and children's bubbly booties too, the shop revolutionizes high quality merchandise at fairly low prices...now that's 'freedom from the usual'!

revolutions_liberty@yahoo.com (Malad)
durgesh_holani@yahoo.com (Nariman Point)

DAILY 11-10

Shop No. 30, InOrbit
Mind Space, Link Road
Malad (W)
Mumbai 400 064
Ph. 91 22 5643 0386
Ph. 91 22 3110 4821

Shop No. 14, CR 2 Mall
Plot No. 240, Backbay
Reclamation, Block 03
Nariman Point
Mumbai 400 021
Ph. 91 22 2311 4820

Rinaldi Design

Rs 1,000 - 7,000

As one of the few designer shoe stores in the country, Rinaldi is not only applauded in India, but abroad as well. Attracting many high-profile clients, this store specializes in bridal footwear. Stone studded belts, zodiac sign t-shirts, and funky watches add to the cache here, while custom-made orders are accepted as well.

rinaldidesigns@aol.com (Parel)
rinaldi50@hotmail.com (Colaba)
www.rinaldidesigns.com

DAILY 11-7.30 (Sun closed)

67/68, Sea View Terrace
118 - B Wodehouse
Road, Colaba
Mumbai 400 005
Ph. 91 22 2215 1394/
2215 2513

308, Kewal Industrial
Estate, S. B. Marg
Lower Parel
Mumbai 400 013
Ph. 91 22 2493 4491/
2206 4561, MAP2 120

Rink's

Rs 800 - 40,000

The selection at this suburban boutique is a mixed bag, ranging from bridal lehengas to western jackets. The denims with a play of corduroys and attractive hand-painted kurtis illustrate the designer's fondness for embroidery and embellishments. In an energetic and playful palette of colours, the clothes are stitched in flowing fabrics, and match the buoyancy and spirit of the shop.

rinkunihalani@hotmail.com

DAILY 11-9 (Sun closed)

6, Kenwood Apartments,
Dr. Ambedkar Road,
Bandra (W),
Mumbai 400 050
Ph. 91 22 3092 8959

Ritu Kumar

Rs 850 onwards

The romance of a Ritu Kumar outfit can be spotted from a distance. Paisley prints with embroidery, and fabrics in earthy tones define her style. A wide collection of ethnic drapery is complemented with purses and scarves; while her prêt line, 'Label' is a rhapsody of threads and silhouettes inspired by fusion culture. The outfits here embody the designer's flair as well as the free-spirited stance of today's youth.

DAILY 10-8

LABEL 5 Sea Palace, 25-H Juhu Tara Road, Juhu
Mumbai 400 049, Ph. 91 22 5692 5346, **MAP1 121**

C211/212, Crossroads, 28,
Pt. M.M. Malviya Road, Haji Ali
Mumbai 400 034
Ph. 91 22 2352 5141

InOrbit Malls- Mindspace
Link Road, Malad (W), Mumbai 400 064
Ph. 91 22 5645 0920

F/52, 2nd floor, Shopping Arcade, The Oberoi
Nariman Point, Mumbai 400 021
Ph. 91 22 2284 6995

Phoenix Block 9, Annexe
Phoenix Mills
462 Senapati Bapat
Marg, Lower Parel
Mumbai 400 013
Ph. 91 22 5666 9901

Akash Ganga
89 Bhulabhai Desai Rd.
Mumbai 400 026
Ph. 91 22 2367 8593

Landmark,
18/A Juhu Tara Road
Juhu, Mumbai 400 049
Ph. 91 22 5697 6983

26 Nariman Shopping
Centre, The Oberoi
Nariman Point, Mumbai
400 021
Ph. 91 22 2287 5975

Rock Fashion Studio

Rs 300 - 15,000

If you ruined your last pair of jeans when you tried to stylishly cut them up, Rock Fashion Studio is the right place to head. There's nothing basic here, the fashion stock here is full of junky club wear ripped tops, army pants and sandblasted jeans. Boots flaming with red threads and wires dangling with miniature skull heads also rust in here, and complete the Metallica look bang on target!

DAILY 11-8.30 (Sun closed)

68 Natraj Co-op
Housing Society
Shop No. 8
Opp. St. Peter's Church
Bandra (W)
Mumbai 400 050
Ph. 91 22 2640 7993

Rockport

Rs 399 - 5,990

An offspring of Reebok, Rockport offers sport shoes for all. Apparels include casuals and denims ideal for mountaineering activities, and camping kits come complete provided with caps and travel bags. A smaller selection of basic tees and Velcro slip-ons also beckon the fairer sex.

U47 InOrbit Mall,
Malad (W),
Mumbai 400 064
Ph. 91 22 56439048/49

28 Linking Road,
Near Mc. Donalds,
Bandra (W),
Mumbai 400 050
Ph. 91 22 2649 8311

DAILY 11-9 (Sun closed)

Rohit Bal

Prices on Request

With an insatiable love for colour, Rohit Bal's forte lies in his strong hand embroidery and eye for detail. His prêt line consists of affordable and wearable clothes complete with crushed cotton lehengas for women and linen jackets for men; while his haute couture has rich-looking formal and bridal wear. Talented, spirited and ever so creative, Bal fashions his lines with proficiency and panache.

S.P. Centre, 10 B
41/ 44 Minoo Desai
Marg, Colaba
Mumbai 400 005
Ph. 91 22 5638 5478/79

info@rohitbal.ws
www.balance.ws

DAILY 11-7.30

Roma

Rs 3,000 onwards

A shop from the Rasulbhai Adamji family, Roma is a high-quality destination for leatherwear and accessories. A special focus on jackets assures a variety of colours and styles to strut, while handbags, hats and leather gloves, make fancy trims to display. A friendly ambience with helpful sales staff, Roma prides in its cannily tailored goods for the crème of society.

46 Colaba Causeway
Near Electric House
Mumbai 400 001
Ph. 91 22 2202 8194

316 Sir JJ Road
Byculla Bridge
Mumbai 400 008
Ph. 91 22 2309 3535

roma316@hotmail.com

DAILY 10.30-7.30 (Sun closed)

Romance

Rs 50 - 1,500

In an otherwise fashion-parched area, this store is a waterhole for accessories. Cosmetics, bracelets, and necklaces ripple around here, while denim handbags swing snazzily in their innovative cuts and washes. Stone pebbled floors with red painted walls camouflage personalized photograph lamps; making this Romance, the perfect place to find a gift for your sweetheart.

Shop No 5,
Kaushik Niwas, LN Road
Matunga (C.R.)
Mumbai 400 019
Ph. 91 22 2411 5100
MAP2 122

DAILY 9.30-8.30 (Mon Closed)

Roman Park

Rs 150 - 8,000

A bit of a misfit in the chaos of the Mulund market, Roman Park carries internationally branded westerns and a range of simple churidar kurtas for men. Accessories available here include ties, undergarments and night suits; making this shop, a worthwhile stop for locals.

DAILY 9-10

R.R.T. Road
Opp. Canara Bank
Mulund (W)
Mumbai 400 080
Ph. 91 22 2560 2527

Roop Milan

Rs 200 - 20,000

Offering a pleasant respite to the endless wandering of sari shops, Roop Milan stacks a variety of casual and bridal wear to suit all budgets. The shop's real USP however, lies in its lehengas and salwar kameezes that offer exclusivity.

inquiry@roopmilan.com
www.roopmilan.com

DAILY 9.30-8.30 (Mon closed)

385 N.C. Kelkar Road
Dadar (W)
Mumbai 400 028
Ph. 91 22 2437 0078/
2431 6574

97 - A Maharshi Karve Road, Marine Lines
Mumbai 400 020
Ph. 91 22 2200 5951

Roop Sangam

Rs 150 - 20,000

After 50 years in business, Roop Sangam knows what sells. Sticking to its roots, this store specializes in traditional saris with ethnic designs, while also frilling its racks with contemporary style saris. Mixing culture with fashion, this emporium stands out for its expansive showroom and large variety of goods.

DAILY 9.30-8.30 (Mon closed)

385 N.C. Kelkar Road
Dadar (W)
Mumbai 400 028
Ph. 91 22 2422 0428

Centre One, S/25 - 26,
Sector 30-A, Vashi
Navi Mumbai 400 705
Ph. 91 22 2781 2244

Roopam

Rs 50 - 1,00,000

Serving to accentuate a woman's enigma and a man's understated panache, Roopam brings fashion to the masses. With an expertise in heavy ethnic and contemporary wear, this store quenches the Indian fetish and placates the western bug. Combining quality and flamboyance, Roopam also offers its NRI clients an e-shopping option.

www.roopam.com

DAILY 9-9

Near Crawford Market
Mumbai 400 002
Ph. 91 22 2206 1794
MAP2 123

Roots

Rs 30 - 1,000

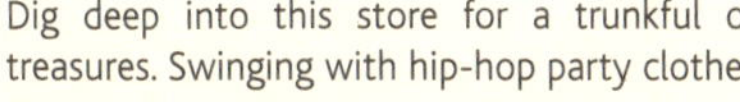
Dig deep into this store for a trunkful of treasures. Swinging with hip-hop party clothes

and daily casuals, the wooden stalks of this fashion-treehouse, make a welcome retreat for fad-frenzied chicas. Hoop earrings and chunky bracelets, dangle along the shop's walls, while funky handbags and cutwork belts, root to be bought.

98 - B, Oomer Park
Opp. St Stephen Church
Warden Road
Mumbai 400 026
Ph. 91 22 2361 1222
MAP2 124

DAILY 10.30-8.30 (Sun closed)

✱ Rouge

Rs 200 - 7,000

Put on your stilettos, dab on some blush and swirl into this ballroom-like store. Seduced sexily against the walls, the spaghetti dresses, flowing chiffon tops, and embroidered jeans, escort you on your first prom night; while quirky slings, ribboned-chokers, and stringy bikinis, offer a sweet joyride to Hawaii. Surely, for a night out or a lippy afternoon luncheon, you have got to put on some red-hot Rouge.

Filmcentre
3rd Floor
Tardeo Road
Mumbai 400 034
Ph. 91 22 2352 0438/ 2352 0439, **MAP2 125**

DAILY 11-7 (Sun closed)

Royal Leather

Rs 400 - 7,000

There is nothing royal about this store, but it provides leather, as you need it. From biker-jackets to leather blazers, you will find every kind of garb in leather here; and what's more... if you can't find your size they will even custom make it for you. Briefcases, belts and wallets are available for men, while knock-off totes and bejewelled Marilyn Monroe tiffin-box purses lure the ladies.

Shop No.3
J.W. Marriot Hotel
Juhu Tara Road
Mumbai 400 049
Ph. 91 22 26941673

58 Oberoi Shopping Centre, Nariman Point
Mumbai 400 021
Ph. 91 22 2285 2399

anand58r@yahoo.com

DAILY 10.30-9.30

✱ Ruff Kids'

Rs 250 - 2,300

If your smashing and dashing kiddo is between 1-16 years of age, this shop is for you! Khakis, linen jackets and checked shirts light up mischievous eyes, while the unisex daring denims stand the naughty mud fights. Beware of the attractive 'Spare Parts' (caps, belts, school bags) though – they make kids drool, begging for more!

Shop No. 106
Heera Panna Shopping Centre, Haji Ali
Mumbai 400 026
Ph. 91 22 2351 2993

Hill Road, Bandra
Mumbai 400 050
Ph. 91 22 2651 0790/ 1
MAP1 126

R Mall, Mulund
Mumbai 400 080
Ph. 91 22 5597 3196

Tram Mandir Road, Thane
Mumbai 400 601
Ph. 91 22 5592 1372

DAILY 10.30-8.30 (Sun closed)

23/24 & 40/41, Chadda Crescent, Sector 17, Vashi
Mumbai 400 705
Ph. 91 22 2766 8436

Rui

Rs 995 - 6,000

Not necessarily fulfilling fashion fantasies, this store keeps clothes that sustain daily practicalities. The embroidered salwar kameezes and kaftans here promise comfort and value-for-money, while the one-off semi-formal outfits strike an occasional stroke of luxury.

DAILY 10.30-7.30 (Sun closed)

Al Dossal, 50 Pali Road
Opp St. Josephs High School, Bandra
Mumbai 400 050
Ph. 91 22 2651 0042 / 2644 2082

Bhagwat Niwas, Gr. Fl.
Opp. Jaslok Hospital
Peddar Road
Mumbai 400 026
Ph. 91 22 2388 2284/ 2386 9343

Sagar

Rs 500 onwards

Elegance and grace predominate a sea of saris here – garments sprinkled with colourful sequins and georgettes lined with embroidered borders look stunning and cater to both casual and festive occasions. Charming its clients with feel-good prices, Sagar has managed to steal many a hearts.

www.sagarsarees.com

DAILY 10-9

502 Jai Mahal
Linking Road, Khar (W)
Mumbai 400 052
Ph. 91 22 2648 5570/ 4225

Jaidev, 33 Road,
Off Linking Road,
Bandra
Mumbai 400 050,
Ph. 91 22 2649 7479/ 2605 8989

Sajid Design Studio

Rs 1,250 - 10,000

Grooms and baraatis, parade in. Welcome to the store that offers a plethora of formal clothing for men. Catering to all personalities, the shop has a range of suits in subtle colours with one-off electric blues and silvers standing out on the racks; while silk formal shirts and sherwanis with delicate embroidery serve to add a gilded touch.

DAILY 11-9.30 (Sun closed)

Joshi House
Opp. Shalimar
Kemps Corner
Mumbai 400 036
Ph. 91 22 2388 6513/ 2382 2059

Sakhi

Rs 1,000 - 20,000

Popular for its saris, Sakhi also has a large variety of simple and poised salwar kameezes and lehengas for women. Adorned with tikkis, stones, and zardozi work, the drapes here come in varied floral and abstract prints. With all the products boasting of supreme quality and fine craftsmanship, the clothes promise to stay your friend through the ages.

sakhiindia@hotmail.com
www.sakhiindia.com

FRI-WED 10-8

Cherryvilla
1st Gauthan Lane
Santacruz (W)
Mumbai 400 054
Ph. 91 22 2605 6551/ 2605 6552

Juhu Tara Road
Opp. Sea Princess
Mumbai 400 049
Ph. 91 22 2661 5555

Salim Asgarally

Rs 1,800 onwards

Very Moroccan, very intriguing... the plum and gold interiors of this couture house will make sure you shop in style. Cocktail dresses, vivacious corsets and crisp linen shirts are perfect to flaunt your plumes in, while exquisite net saris and an elaborate bridal collection makes the haute couture sensational here. Don't miss the bejewelled lamps, velvet cushions and antique couches – quite comfy, when you arrange an appointment with the designer himself!

salimasgarally@gmail.com
www.salimasgarally.com

DAILY 10.30-8.30 (Sun closed)

99 Abde Ville
SV Road, Khar (W)
Mumbai 400 052
Ph. 91 22 5629 5265/66
MAP1 127

Sambena

Rs 300 - 4,000

Recreating every season's style as it happens, Sambena offers affordable bags 'you'll love to shoulder'. An ambitious range of styles from party clutch-ons to college-cool totes is featured here, while spin-offs and in-house collections are spruced up with natty trimmings and fancy buckles. From clichéd to cocky, you will find it all here.

mateen@sambena.com
www.sambena.com

DAILY 10.30-8.30 (Sun closed)

21, Cusrow Baug
Colaba
Mumbai 400 036
Ph. 91 22 2284 3739

6 Joshi House
Kemps Corner
Mumbai 400 036
Ph. 91 22 2387 2978
MAP2 128

Samsonite

Rs 2,500 - 25,000

Although most popular for its luggage, this world-renowned brand also has a small collection of slings, worthy of mention. Bags in heterogeneous shapes and sizes make their mark here, while bright wallets and pouches add multicoloured frills. More basic than fashionable, Samsonite's supreme quality assures its clients a long-term commitment.

crossroads@samsonite.co.in

DAILY 10.30-8.30

Samsonite Travel World, S.V. Road
Near Standard Chartered Bank, Santacruz (W)
Mumbai 400 054
Ph. 91 22 2661 5863

Samsonite Travel World, 4/ B Hasan Manzil
Opp. Nish Chinese Restaurant, Kemps Corner
Mumbai 400 036
Ph. 91 22 2380 6912

Crossroads
Shop No. C - 310/ 11
28, Pandit M.M. Malviya Road, Haji Ali,
Mumbai 400 034
Ph. 91 22 5662 4085/ 5660 8160

R.R.T Road, Mulund (W)
Mumbai 400 080
Ph. 91 22 5555 0438

Nawab Building
323 Dr. D.M. Road Fort
Mumbai 400 001
Ph. 91 22 2283 8576/ 2204 8764

Sayonara Nagesh
622 Mohan Mahal
Linking Road
Opp. Khar MTNL
Khar (W)
Mumbai 400 052
Ph. 91 22 2600 5182/ 2600 6185

Maru Centre, S.V. Road, Opp. Shoppers' Stop
Andheri (W), Mumbai 400 053
Ph. 91 22 2671 8834

VIP Maru, Abhishek Building, S.V. Road
Opp. Malad Shopping Centre, Near Dena Bank
Malad (W), Mumbai 400 064
Ph. 91 22 2881 3313

179 Waterfield Road, Linking Road, Bandra (W)
Mumbai 400 050
Ph. 91 22 5696 4841

Vashi Plaza, Vashi
Mumbai 400 703
Ph. 91 22 2781 2027

Choksi Mansion, Dr. Ambedkar Road
Next to Reebok, Parel,
Mumbai 400 012
Ph. 91 22 2418 7173

Shop No. 4, Haveli Apartments,Chandawarkar Crossroad, Borivali (W), Mumbai 400 092
h. 91 22 2801 7395

Satya Paul

Rs 2,200 - 30,000

Chicly hand-painted and printed fabrics make a distinct style statement for an era that dares to remix the traditional with the abstract. Saris swing gracefully in their inimitable designs, while kurtis and ties flaunt their chromatic strokes. It's no surprise that stylish 'Mallika Ma'm' of the 'Jassi Jaisi Koi Nahin' fame flaunts a new Satya Paul creation every episode; after all every printed drape tells a different story.

DAILY 11-8

C 204/205 Crossroads
28, Pt. M.M. Malviya
Road, Haji Ali
Mumbai 400 034
Ph. 91 22 5660 3880

Near Be: Kemps Corner
Mumbai 400 026
Ph. 91 22 3951 0612/
2380 5239, MAP2 129

30B High Tide Road
Juhu Tara Road
Mumbai 400 049
Ph. 91 22 3094 8002

Saundarya

Rs 700 - 7,000

Beautiful wooden interiors house Indian and indo-western clothing for women, at this hole-in-the-wall. Block printed with handwork, on offer here are light lehengas, salwar kameezes and night suits. Available in a variety of designs, the affordable garbs here allow women to look beautiful without having to loosen their purse strings.

TUE-SUN 10-10

69 B
3 - A Janardhan Chhaya
Sathe Park, 19 Road
Chembur
Mumbai 400 071
Ph. 91 22 2528 7548

Scandal

Rs 390 - 4,275

Like it or not, fashion is still seduced by the stiletto; and here is one shop with stilettos galore! Specializing in acrylic heels, this store also racks a variety of formal and sporty shoes for men and children. Also stocking international brands, Scandal brings diverse varieties of products – all at un-scandalous prices.

scandal-india@yahoo.com

DAILY 10.30-9.30

512 Linking Road
Near National College
Bandra (W)
Mumbai 400 050
Ph. 91 22 2604 9703/
2604 9711

Scram

Rs 275 - 395

Here is yet another reason for naughty kids to behave. Scram has rubber printed shirts with sporty designs for young boys and t-shirts with flowers and added shimmer for little girls. Capris, three-fourths and frilled skirts tiptoe in here too, while athletic goodies scram to be bought for super-active kids.

DAILY 11-10

Shop F12, 1st Floor
In Orbit Mall, Link Road
Malad, Mumbai 400 064
Ph. 91 22 5645 0939

311 Mehta Building
Ground Floor
Next to Caesars Palace
12th Road, Khar
Mumbai 400 052
Ph. 91 22 3951 9050

SD Lounge

Rs 599 - 999

Clothes so comfy you'll want to sleep. Combed cottons printed with soothing pastels make sleeveless vests, while relaxed shorts and summer time capris make lazy afternoon siestas. Expect to find snug outfits that keep you comfy under vanilla skies and matching coffee mugs and flip-flops that sweeten up pillow fights. A great place to find international quality sleep and lounge wear.

DAILY 10.30-9.30

U16 InOrbit Mall
Malad (W)
Mumbai 400 064
Ph. 91 22 5698 0546

Selection Centre

Rs 50 - 500

Lost amidst its neighbouring sports stores, Selection Centre has casual sports and fitness wear for everyone, including your Beckham-crazy four year old. Jerseys, shorts, swimwear, and internationally branded shoes make up the entire selection, while disappointed patrons can always walk over to the Fila showroom – one shop away – for greater variety.

sports@bom3.vsnl.net.in
www.selectionsports.com

DAILY 10.30-8.30 (Sun closed)

Charman Chambers
Next to Metro
A.P. Marg, Dhobi Talao
Mumbai 400 020
Ph. 91 22 2203 4097/
2209 4509

Shakun

Rs. 700-1,00,000

Bandhanis, leheriyas and gharchoras flood this family-run boutique in all their vibrant colours and patterns. Saris, dupattas and fabrics that are reminiscent of auspicious festivities promise to truly liven up your celebrations. Shakun also keeps an exquisite range of Patolas from Patan in Gujarat.

www.shakunbandhani.com

DAILY 10-7 (Sun closed)

3 Marshall Apartments
97, August Kranti Marg
Kemps Corner
Mumbai 400 036
Ph. 91 22 5600 9943 /
2388 1203

Sheetal

Rs 200 onwards

An all-purpose fashion store, Sheetal has a great variety of glittery dresses, casual cotton shirts and semi-formal suits for all occasions. Traditional collections from high-profile designers add a tinsel-tint to the shop's booty, while the imitation jewellery silver-line the walls. Fashionable babies can get dressed in here too.

www.sheetalindia.com

DAILY 10-9 (Sun closed)

56 L.T. Road
Crawford Market
Mumbai 400 002
Ph. 91 22 2206 1016/ 6969, MAP2 **130**

Sheetal Design Studio

Rs 495 - 23,000

Designed by Aki Narula and Hemant Trivedi, the party-wear printed shirts and linen kurtas for men stand out in their cuts and designs; while the in-house range of sequin bordered saris and modish tops spell out sophistication and class. For a bubbly champagne lunch or a Bacardi night out, pop in for some fizz.

sheetal@bom3.vsnl.net.in
www.sheetalindia.com

DAILY 10.30-9 (Sun closed)

18 Bhulabhai Desai Road
Opp. Tirupati Apartments
Mumbai 400 026
Ph. 91 22 2351 9728/ 2351 9977, MAP2 **131**

Sheetal Estate
Grant Road
Mumbai 400 007
Ph. 91 22 2385 6565

Shehenaz

Rs 50 onwards

This modest store stands out for its colourful collections of imitation and silver jewellery. Bedecking its walls is a kaleidoscope of beaded necklaces, earrings and pendants; while mirror-work handbags, belts and bindis, all make reasonable buys. Popular with tourists, this store sells with its wares, a feel of rural India.

shahenazexports@hotmail.com
www.shahenazexports.com

DAILY 10-8

3, Oberoi Shopping Arcade
The Oberoi,
Nariman Point,
Mumbai 400 021
Ph. 91 22 2288 0506 / 6929

Shilpa K

Rs 1,500 - 9,000

Tucked away in the hoi polloi of Maker Arcade, Shilpa K is worth the hunt. Catering to all ages, the store's designs are trendy yet comfortable, with easily manageable styles. Embroidered kurtis and salwars with unique embellishments cater to its middle-aged clientele, while trendy linen tops, crushed ghagra skirts and chiffon ponchos add a youthful zing to the store's ready-to-wear collection.

shilpa@shilpak.com

DAILY 10-7.30 (Sun closed)

87 Maker Arcade,
Cuffe Parade,
Mumbai 400 005
Ph. 91 22 2218 4600
MAP2 **132**

Shlok

Rs 900 - 50,000

Housing creations from the likes of Manish Malhotra, Rohit Bal and Sabhyasachi Mukherjee, Shlok is a chanted shopping mantra for page three celebs. With bohemian pants and shelled-skirts, button-down kurtas and pearl-laden saris, the shop emits ebullience and poise. Its reasonably priced shirt collection from 'Liquid' however, is the real hot-sell, while Edwin Pinto's shoes and embroidered handbags from Kolkata jazz up the glad rags.

DAILY 11-8

Quorum
Shop No. 11
Phoenix Mill 462
Senapati Bapat Marg
Lower Parel
Mumbai 400 013
Ph. 91 22 5661 0428

Shoppers' Stop

Rs 50 onwards

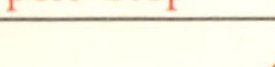   

Their formula is fashion and quality, at acceptable prices. Catering to everyone from bratty boys to graceful grandmamas, Shoppers' Stop covers all the ranks. Whether it is a scheduled visit or an impulsive urge, you can always build an appetite for the products at this store. Your shopping extravaganza can now finish with a delicious end at the in-store Baristas, present in most branches.

DAILY 10.30-8.30

41 Naman Plaza, Opp. Thatai Bhatia Hall
Shanker Lane S.V. Road, Kandivili (W), Mumbai 400 067,
Ph. 91 22 2801 2890

InOrbit Mall Malad, Mindspace Link Road Malad (W)
Mumbai 400 064
Ph. 91 22 5643 4700 / 01 / 02

211-D.S.V. Road
Andheri (W)
Mumbai – 400058
Ph. 91 22 2624 0451/ 55

Krushal Commercial Complex, M.G. Road
Near Chembur Station Flyover
Mumbai 400 079
Ph. 91 22 2527 5802

Suburbia (Old Bandra Talkies), Linking Road
Bandra (W)
Mumbai 400 050.
Ph. 91 22 2643 5424
MAP1 133

Nirmal Lifestyle, L.B.S Marg, Mulund (W)
Mumbai 400 080,
Ph. 91 22 2593 5001

Shringar

Rs 1,000 onwards

A blink-and-miss-it store, Shringar lies cosily between its more popular neighbours. Low-key and modest, the shop specializes in western clothing for men while also keeping a moderate range of saris, lehengas and kurtis for women. The last-minute custom made service available here is handy.

DAILY 10-9 (Sun closed)

Kemps Corner
Opp. Shalimar Hotel
Mumbai 400 036
Ph. 91 22 2388 0650/ 5600 1577

Shruti

Rs 650 - 5,500

Silently serving its clients for 15 years, Shruti has an extremely wearable collection of Indian casuals. Embroidered salwar kameezes and pin-tucked kurtis make comfortable work days,

1, Guide Building,
Napean Sea Road,
Mumbai 400 006
Ph. 91 22 2363 6650

while printed kaftans offer leisure within the house. The interplay with various fabrics here, create a range of clothing suitable for daily wash-n-wear.

DAILY 10-9 (Sun closed)

Shyam Ahuja

Rs 350 onwards

India's most famous dhurrie maker, Shyam Ahuja is known for his outstandingly handcrafted products. Home furnishings in vivid colours include table linens, bathrobes, and towels. Most of the products here are made from natural fibres and in earthy colours, and you can also find yourself some authentic pashmina shawls!

shyamahuja@vsnl.com

DAILY 10-7.30 (Sun closed)

Opp. Murphy Radio, Hajuri Road, Off Eastern Express Highway, Thane, Mumbai 400 601
Ph. 91 22 25822155/ 2549

Near Vama Road
Peddar Road
Mumbai 400 026
Ph. 91 22 2386 7372
MAP2 134

Gazdar Apts 'C' Wing
Juhu Tara Road, Juhu
Mumbai 400 049
Ph. 91 22 2615
2140 / 1749

Si Branché

Rs 550 - 7,000

If you plan on sizzling the dance floor the next time you go out partying, make sure you visit this shop. Smocked jersey skirts, tight spaghettis with even tighter pants will make you look oh-so-sexy, while trendy gym gear with cross-backed tops, will sweat to make you look even sexier. The chichi earrings and knock-off bags complete the party mood, while men can get a more sophisticated re-do with formal jackets and leather shoes.

sibranche@hotmail.com

DAILY 12-9.30, SUN 3-9

10/11 Kenwood
Apartments
Dr. Ambedkar Road
Bandra (W)
Mumbai 400 050
Ph. 91 22 2604 6722

Sia

Rs 195 - 18,000

This chain of shops offers an exquisite range of silver and gold plated fashion jewellery, with antique finished topaz-hued bridal sets and traditional Bikarneri jadaos. The regalia present here brings alive the romance of the palaces, while magnificent maangtikas and august tiaras, crown you queen!

DAILY 11-8

InOrbit Mall, Malad, Mumbai 400 064
Ph. 91 22 3095 2972

Surang Shopping Centre
Santacruz (W)
Mumbai 400 054
Ph. 91 22 2605 3068

Kemps Corner
Mumbai 400 026
Ph. 91 22 2381 2628
MAP2 135

Matunga
Mumbai 400 019
Ph. 91 22 2404 3321

Borivali (W),
Mumbai 400 091
Ph. 91 22 2861 7755

Sidewalks of the World

Rs 695 onwards

An opium pipe from Burma, Aztec pottery from Peru, and a Samurai sword from Japan –following a global theme, this store keeps artefacts that add a touch of snob value to your home. Apart from lavish furniture, a variety of handicrafts that range from art deco to Zen are available here. The designer also takes on projects for decorating private spaces.

34 Walchand Hirachand Marg
Ballard Estate
Mumbai 400 030
Ph. 91 22 2261 4733

MON-FRI 10.30-7.30, SAT 10.30-7

Sign O' Times

Rs 275 - Rs 3,000

Due to labels like Diesel and Tommy Hilfiger, this up-to-the-minute shop has gained timeless popularity. A small range of block printed tie-ups and sequinned kurtis add an indo-western touch while the naughty cartoon ties for men gusto up the hunky end.

At Ortens Enterprises
239 Hortencia
Junction of Linking Road
30th Road, Bandra (W)
Mumbai 400 050
Ph. 91 22 2645 3481

DAILY 10.30-8.30

Silver Age

Rs 700 onwards

The trifles at Silver Age will please patrons scraping for some metal. More traditional than contemporary, the baubles available here are bejewelled with solitaires, icy sparklers and amber aces. Antique jadao sets also treasure alongside sling pendants; providing customers diverse selections at moderate prices.

Near Benzer
Bhulabhai Desai Road
Mumbai 400 026

✹ Skin Sin

Rs 1900 - 6000

Calling out to all the fashionable femmes who are bold enough to drop their inhibitions, and indulge in some materialistic sins. Skin Sin believes in keeping the Indian woman up-to-date with international trends and pampers her with shoe styles varying in toe shapes, heel heights and textures. Dominating her outfit, and lightening her walk, this brand confirms that beauty is indeed skin deep.

Grand Hyatt Mumbai
Off Western Express Highway
Santacruz (East)
Mumbai 400 055
Ph. 91 22 5676 1234

Sleep-ins

Rs 595 onwards

With internationally styled sleep and lounge wear, Sleep-ins stocks snoozy pjs, capris and shorts in drowsy colours. The bridal nightwear available in flirty shades will zoom

Shop No. 108, Level 1
Cross Roads
Near Haji Ali, Tardeo
Mumbai 400 034
Ph. 91 22 3090 7062

you straight to dreamland; while all the night suits are relaxed in their fits and prices.

MON-SAT 10.30-8.30, SUN 11.30-8.30

Sole to Soul

Rs 600 - 2,500

Souls searching for unique solemates are invited to this double-storeyed shoe house. A refreshing respite from regular designs, Sole to Soul has great coordinates for deserving peds. Lime green stilettos, kitten-heeled kolhapuris and towering boots satisfy all shoe-o-holic fantasies. And if you cannot find a perfect match, get it cloned here to your desire!

532, Kudpi House,
Linking Road,
Mumbai 400 052
Ph. 91 22 5677 8422
MAP1 130

DAILY 10.30-9.30 (Sun closed)

Soshé

Rs 599 - 4,990

Move over New York and Milan, give way to Soshé! From net tops and laced pants to charm sandals and quirky jewellery, everything here has an international flavour with a nutty twist. Tolerably priced, but uncompromising on its quality, this store is a bang-on destination for a girl who knows what she wants.

Shop 1, Beach Haven
Next to Hotel Ramada
Inn, Juhu
Mumbai 400 049
Ph. 91 22 2615 1756/
2618 0469

DAILY 11-8.30 (Sun closed)

Spykar Jeans

Rs 175 - 1,395

Specializing in jeans and casual wear, Spykar proudly proclaims that it is more fashion-savvy than its competitors. Catering to the chewing-gum brigade, the brand spies on the latest trends and captures them all at justifiable prices. Beware of the brand's 'Rebel' collection, it threatens to reform the new generation's style dictum.

MON-SAT 11-9, Sun 11-9.30

Adventure Fashion, S.V. Road, Dahisar, Mumbai 400 068
Ph. 91 22 2892 6229

Divyan Collections, J.B. Nagar, Andheri (E)
Mumbai 400 058, Ph. 91 22 2832 5447

Jay Retailing, Marine Lines Station, Marine Lines
Mumbai 400 020, Ph. 91 22 2205 8827

Shop No. 8, Sky Zone
Phoenix Mill Compound
Lower Parel
Mumbai 400 013
Ph. 91 22 5661 1383/
2492 5671

Piramyd Mega Store
2nd Floor, Cross Roads
Haji Ali
Mumbai 400 026
Ph. 91 22 2351
5890 / 5894

Span Apparels
Shop No. 207, 2nd Floor
Opp. Zee Telefilms
Andheri (E)
Mumbai 400 059
Ph. 91 22 5675 0701/02

K.C. College, Churchgate
Mumbai 400 007
Ph. 91 22 5631 5504/05

Star Sports

Rs 290 - 2,890

Not the sports channel we see on TV, this store however aspires to capture a bit of that

4, 5-Chaman Chambers
AP Road

sporting spirit. Ranging from tennis rackets to skateboards, the shop also stocks a small selection of basic sportswear. Football studs, spiked shoes and skates whiz by in all sizes, while socks and headbands brace up for the finish line.

DAILY 10-9, SUN 10-1

Dhobi Talao
Mumbai 400 020
Ph. 91 22 2206 1717/
2208 2315

Street Markets

Rs 25 - 500

A bhel-puri of kitschy clothing, accessories and footwear, the street markets of Mumbai cannot be missed when walking down the city's fashion lanes. Amidst the 'cutting-chai' and crackling light bulbs, the motley stalls in winding alleys hustle and bustle with squabbling locals and speechless tourists. Chock-a-block with junk jewellery, scrappy stilettos, and threadbare tunics, these thela-walas thrive on impulsive-buys and thrilling bargain-bets. However, before buying your alluring product, make sure you bargain strongly – quote half the demanded price to start with.

DAILY, TIMINGS VARY

The Galleria, Powai
Mumbai 400 076
Best Buys: Footwear

Lokhandwala,
Andheri
Mumbai 400 013
Best Buys: Clothes, Footwear

Fashion Street, Fort
Mumbai 400 023
Best Buys: Jeans

Colaba Causeway
Mumbai 400 005
Best Buys: Jewellery, Sunglasses

Crawford Market
Mumbai 400 003
Best Buys: Cosmetics, Household Goods

Linking Road
Bandra
Mumbai 400 052
Best Buys: Footwear

Bhuleshwar
Mumbai 400 004
Best Buys: Traditional Jewellery

Hill Road, Bandra (W),
Mumbai 400 050
Best Buys: Clothes

Studio F

Rs 50 - 3,000

The fashion-sense here halts at the F of fashion. Racking a range of halter knits, frilled tops, embroidered pants, and a small collection of men's kurtas; this store prides itself in its well priced handbags and accessories.

DAILY 10.30-7 (Sun closed)

Ram - Nimi Building
Mandlik Road, Colaba
Mumbai 400 001
Ph. 91 22 5634 5555

✷ Studio Lingerie

Rs 1,500 - 6,000

Delicately exquisite and exorbitantly priced, Studio Lingerie only stocks the French brand, Aubade. From lacy feminines to mischievous seductresses, every possible boudoir sensibility is represented here. Trendsetters in brevity, this avant-garde brand still handworks every stitch, and frills every lace for a genuinely personalized touch. G-string, boxers, t-shirt

Quorum, 1st floor
High Street Phoenix
462 Senapati Bapat
Marg, Lower Parel
Mumbai 400 013
Ph. 91 22 5660 8970

bras and bikinis...Men, these are what fantasies are made of!

ftcindia@tiscali.fr

DAILY 11-8

Studio M

Rs 2,000 - 20,000

A boutique store by Indian shoe giant Metro, Studio M presents products exclusively for men. Madhubani canvas-painted shoes by Rohit Bal, stylized leather mojris by Manish Malhotra and high cowboy boots are a few of the shop's stellar peds; while international brands like Bally and Skechers ensure suitable 'foot escorts' for any occasion.

Below Mc Donald's,
Linking Road,
Bandra,
Mumbai 400 052
Ph. 91 22 5656 0444
MAP1 137

DAILY 10-10.30

Studio Prêt

Rs 500 - 8,000

With styles flowing straight from the haughty catwalks to the wearable sidewalks, this casual corner presents a keen collection of diffusion designer lines. Tunics with pop-art motifs, embroidered ponchos and drapery style dresses make a voguish entry at girly dim-sum lunches, while flirtatious chiffons add gaiety and flair to the femme fashion spirit.

Ground Floor,
Vasundhara Building
5 Bhulabhai Desai Road
Mumbai 400 026
Ph. 91 22 2351 6459

DAILY 10.30-7 (Sun closed)

Studio Sajid

Rs 1,850 - 10,000

Nothing is just black and white; there are off-whites too. Sajid Studio Design's simple and modest brother, this shop has casual clothing exclusively in whites, off-whites and a few whisks of blacks. Famous for its appliqué work, the shop offers salwar kameezes, churidars, and indo-western kurtis in textured cotton fabrics; all giving off a breezy and unruffled look.

Nawaz Court
Kemps Corner
Mumbai 400 036
Ph. 91 22 2382 2059

studiosajid@hotmail.com

DAILY 11-9.30 (Sun closed)

Studio Sinitta

Rs 200 - 30,000

With a relaxed Mediterranean ambience, this store serves a range of casual and party western wear. Most popular for their groom's collection, the in-house designers decorate

2 Mani Mansion
63 Peddar Road
Mumbai 400 026
Ph. 91 22 2385 5887/
2385 5760

kurtas with heavy embroidery and offer formal suits in clean cuts. Printed tops, body-fit halters, and flimsy skirts greet the ladies, while belts and scarves finish the look.

shrimankerkaushik@hotmail.com

DAILY 10-8 (Sun closed)

Style Mantra

Rs 500 - 3,000

Featuring well-priced clothing for babes who can hold 'breathtaking' attires, this shop has everything from fitting tops and cropped jeans to party dresses and winter jackets. Unleashing funky fashion sense, the imported shoes and matching handbags here also jump-start the sweet-and-sexy look in a dash.

DAILY 11-9

19 Jethabhai Building
Bomanji Petit Road
Opp. Warden Road
Parsi Gen. Hosp. Lane
Mumbai 400 036
Ph. 91 22 2364 2377
MAP2 138

7 Shktiraj CHS,
Next to HSBC,
Pali Road, Bandra (W),
Mumbai 400 050
Ph. 91 22 2634 7764/
5677 7409

Suneet Varma

Rs 13,000 onwards

Get ready for some high-octave glam; with sassy Suneet Varma who believes in celebrating femininity with his luminious gladrags. Innovative placements and striking contrasts scintillate salwars and saris, while lehengas lavishly glaze the bridal wear. Grooms' attires can also be pre-arranged with appointments from the designer.

courtyard@vsnl.net

DAILY 11-7.30
(For trousseau appointments only)

The Courtyard,
S.P. Centre,
41/44 Minoo Desai
Marg, Colaba,
Mumbai 400 005
Ph. 91 22 5638 5462/63

Sun-Way Leather House

Rs 100 - 20,000

Don't be cowed down by the variety of bags found at this shop, which could overwhelm the needs of any buyer. Handbags in every avatar can be found here, to suit the idiosyncracies of any outfit or personality. Deep within this warehouse however, lie stone and zari work pouches that aspire to provide customers with a gilded break from other passé products.

DAILY 10-8.30

Maskati Corner
Altamount Road
Kemps Corner
Mumbai 400 036
Ph. 91 22 2386 9893
MAP2 139

Sushobhit

Rs 2,000 onwards

Muted interiors set-off heavily embroidered traditional wear in earthy tones and natural fibres. Specializing in trousseau and ethnic wear, this shop provides sherwanis and dhotis for men; while the rustic

Poddar House,
Ground Floor,
'A' Road, Marine Drive,
Mumbai 400 020
Ph. 91 22 2287 3334
MAP2 140

femmes are treated with culture-clad lehengas and saris. Children can also be taken back in time with ethnic wear orders accepted here.

investpa@vsnl.com
www.sushobhit.com

DAILY 9.45-6.30 (Sun closed)

Svago

Rs 595 - 2,500

Slip on a pair of yellow pom-pom sandals and swagger into Svago. Scraping to sustain itself from neighbouring competition, this shoe store has maintained its niche identity, à la, its occasional collection of unique designs. Priding in its wide range of 'inspired' footwear, the store sponsors many TV soaps; fulfilling all the temperamental 'Saas-Bahu' demands.

No.2, Kudpi House,
Linking Road,
Bandra,
Mumbai 400 050
Ph. 91 22 5697 0942

DAILY 11-9

Swarovski

Rs 1,600 - 15,000

Diamonds are a girl's best friend; the next best chum is Swarovski. Synonymous with crystals world over, this accredited brand trickles superior craftsmanship with graceful designs. Sparkling out an array of earrings, bracelets, neckpieces and handbags, Swarovski is the perfect way to star-stud an occasion or aglow a wardrobe. To tinsel up the look further, Swarovski also offers crystal body tattoos; who says beauty isn't skin deep?

231 Link Corner Building
Shop No. 3, Linking
Road, Bandra (W)
Mumbai 400 034
Ph. 91 22 2640 2510
MAP1 141

C/ 219-222 Crossroads
28 Pandit Malviya Road
Haji Ali
Mumbai 400 034
Ph. 91 22 5660 2120/23

DAILY 10.30-9

Shop No. 25- 26, Crossroads 2,
Nariman Point, Mumbai 400 021
Ph. 91 22 5655 0932/0933

S'warya

Rs 800 - 17,000

A comforting alternative to high street labels, this recent entrant offers upmarket clothing at lower prices. Classic westerns with brocade and appliqué are stylized to form halters-tops and shirts here; while georgettes and crepes inflated with sequins and zardozi work make versatile saris and dress materials.

B-1 Jains Arcade,
14th Road,
Khar (W),
Mumbai 400 052
Ph. 91 22 3096 9173

karishmajaisingh@hotmail.com

DAILY 11-6 (Sun closed)

Tangerine

Rs 40 - 2,000

Boys are rotten made of cotton, girls are handy made of candy – but at Tangerine the two gangs can frisk goodies together. Cooing out to 0-14 year olds, this tangy shop has everything from cartoon printed capris to formal sherwanis. Made of cotton, the comfortable clothes at this store aspire to make your kiddos look as sweet as candy.

1 Krishnabad
43 Bhulabhai Desai Rd
Mumbai 400 026
Ph. 91 22 2352 5673/74

tangerine_kids@yahoo.com

DAILY 10.30-8.30 (Sun closed)

Tango

Rs 50 - 2,000

Tangerine's older sibling, Tango offers casual western wear for all. Constantly unfurled by enthusiastic salesmen, the stacked up shirts, bottoms and windcheaters here, make acceptable daily 'throw-and-go's'. More for blending in than for getting noticed, the shop's products have good quality; all at tango prices.

493 Linking Road
Bandra
Mumbai 400 050
Ph. 91 22 2649 9971

FRI-WED 10.30-8.30

Tarun Tahiliani

Prices on Request

Arched ceilings literally dripping with crystals, Tarun Tahiliani's shop resembles a princely boudoir. Lined with whimsical salwar kameezes and belted linen overcoats, this walk-in closet also suits pin tuck sherwanis and sharply tailored pants for men. Specializing in fusion work, Tahiliani skilfully montages noodle tops with saris and western shirts with paisley prints. A private 'Sheesh-Mahal' is dedicated to personal client meetings and trousseau appointments. Kudos to this shop, which is as much an artwork as its treasures.

Villar Ville, Gr. Floor
16 Ramchandani Marg
Apollo Bunder
Mumbai 400 039
Ph. 91 22 2287 0895/
2285 4603, MAP2 142

ahilian@bom5.vsnl.net.in
www.taruntahiliani.com

DAILY 11-7 (Sun closed)

Telon

Rs 700 onwards

Wrought-iron meshes set a handsome ambience for this shop steeped in heavy tradition. Coutured sherwanis, classic trousers and textured suits weigh their presence here, while smart club wear shirts sling on with youthful vim. The cuts are conventional, the fabrics wide-ranging, and the details engaging.

149 Doctor Building,
Kemps Corner,
Mumbai 400 026
Ph. 91 22 2367 9997/
2367 5554, MAP1 143

The Kemps Corner branch offers a more lavish experience in terms of choice and ambience.

telon@bom3.vsnl.net.in

DAILY 10-9

35 Hill Road,
Opp. Elco Market,
Bandra,
Mumbai 400 050
Ph. 91 22 2643 8733/
2643 8716

Tent

Rs 150 - 2,000

It is not often that you would find a clothes camp with therapeutic pillows and dream-catchers, but such is the eclectic character of this tent. The spirit here is young and erratic with outlandish tops, sexy sarongs, and beach hot pants making sultry Goa evenings even hotter; while funky flip-flops besides Feng-Shui yin-yangs zing in a holistic lifestyle.

t_thadani@hotmail.com
www.tentsphere.com

DAILY 11-8 (Sun closed)

2A Meherabad,
Bhulabhai Desai Road,
Mumbai 400 026
Ph. 91 22 2369 6173

The Bombay Stores

Rs 110 - 10,000

Immerse yourself in 95 years of Indian folklore at The Bombay Stores. Complete with wooden flooring and tall ceilings, this store has a wide array of western and Indian outfits for all ages. Mosaiced with hand-knotted jewellery and leather handbags, this colonial edifice also parades shoes, stoles and hats. A modernistic flavour added on with a few international brands, this store successfully mixes tradition with fashion.

vishals@bombaystore.com
www.thebombaystore.com

DAILY 10.30-7.30

Western India House
Sir P.M. Road
Mumbai 400 001
Ph. 91 22 2288 5048/
2288 5049, **MAP2 144**

Domestic Airport
Terminal 1B
Mumbai
Ph. 91 22 2615 6515

The Champion Sports

Rs 100 - 500

This shop offers a sturdy selection of athletic assortments, along with Speedo swimwear and accessories. Colours remain solid and simple, favouring function over form; while reasonable prices make shopping here a cinch.

DAILY 10.30-8 (Sun closed)

Jehangir Mansion,
AP Road, Dhobi Talao,
Mumbai 400 020
Ph. 91 22 2203 1235

The Courtyard

Rs 650 onwards

Rumoured to give exclusivity a new definition, The Courtyard has added to Mumbai's map a new destination for luxury shopping. Nestled in a Colaba heritage estate, this beautifully landscaped piazza is occupied by top-notch fashion designers and home décor stores; while Adhuna Akhtar's hair salon Juice and celebrity chef and restaurateur, Dino Martelli's Café Sesso completes the indulgence. So go ahead and soak yourself in sumptuousness, hauteur and extravagance.

S.P. Centre
41/ 44 Minoo Desai
Marg, Colaba
Mumbai 400 005

DAILY 10.30-8.30

Refer to the following stores for further details:

Abraham & Thakore, Ashish N Soni, Ego
Manish Arora/ Fish Fry, Narendra Kumar, Pratap
Rabani & Rakha, Rohit Bal, Suneet Varma, Tulsi

The Double Bull Wagon

Rs 700 - 8,000

More basic than bold, the selections here cover all dressing essentials. Men can find everything for both, their weekday and weekend wardrobes, with particular emphasis laid on Italian-fit suits and casual wear. The smaller selection of women's and children's garbs fit the same 'ordinary' sensibility; all at 'cannot-get-better' prices.

DAILY 10-8.30 (Colaba) DAILY 10-9 (Bandra)

Regal Cinema Building,
Chhatrapati Shivaji
Marg, Colaba,
Mumbai 400 039
Ph. 91 22 2202 0524/
1815

Servesh Sadan,
Linking Road,
Bandra (W),
Mumbai 400 050
Ph. 91 22 2642 7905/
2640 357

The Indian Textiles Company

Rs 2,000 - 90,000

This luxurious showroom stacked with ornate saris and shawls presents exclusive selections of fine Banarsi jamdanis and antique brocades. Apart from the specialities available here, the contemporary crepes and flowing chiffons spruce up the shop's displays with sashaying style. For a textile voyage through Indian lands, make sure you dock at this sari shore.

www.indian-textiles.com

DAILY 11.30-7.30 (Sun closed)

The Taj Mahal Hotel
Apollo Bunder
Mumbai 400 001
Ph. 91 22 2283 0030/37
MAP2 145

* The Jewellery Plaza

Rs 100 - 5,000

Few shops these days can lay claim to a truly unique selection, but this is one of them. Treasuring magnific jewels to prettify every outfit, the baubles here range from delicate silver trinkets and bling-bling bracelets to chunky pendants and charmed waistbelts. Cherrying beauties with grace and flair, this expansive Plaza has much to share. So whisp in, for some tangle-free jingle and jangle.

mails@thejewelleryplaza.com

DAILY 9-9

Plot No. 27
Gulmohar Road
Ground Floor,
Saurashtra Soc.
JVPD Scheme
Near Juhu Lokhandwala
Circle, Vile Parle (W)
Mumbai 400 049
Ph. 91 22 5698 9373

The Juniors Shoppe

Rs 15 - 8,000

Tiny in size, just like its target client, this store caters to grubby-kneed kiddies. Formerly a toy house, the natty collections here, now also includes rompers and denim dresses, for its nappy-clients. The shoppe's cute clothes promise comfort and relaxation to your tiny-tots, or rather, to you.

mytoyco@rediffmail.com
juniors_shoppe@rediffmail.com

DAILY 10-8.30 (Sun closed)

Suite No. 5, 2nd Floor
Tayyabji Building
262 L.T Marg
Opp. G. T. Hospital
Mumbai 400 002
Ph. 91 22 2207 7319/ 8783, 2200 7514/ 5635 0738, **MAP2 146**

✺ The Loft

Rs 50 - 20,000

Imagine a monstrous double-decked loft; now fill it up with shoes, shoes and more shoes. A shopping haven for shoe-o-holics, The Loft, is a melting caldron of over 150 brands. Ranging from Fendi and Harley Davidson to Rinaldi and Bata; the thumb rule here is to serve any toe-size that twiddles in. Strutting an upmarket look and asking for crawling prices in return, this giant makes the trudge up here, worth every step of the way.

DAILY 11-9

Level Two
Haiko Mall
Powai
Mumbai 400 076
Ph. 91 22 5693 9777
MAP1 147

The Loot

Rs 299 - 6,400

If you are not fussed about a pair of Levi's jeans with the wrong coloured seam, or a Reebok top without the tag, you are headed the right way. The store retails sports and casual wear of 30 brands with minor defects 'at up to 60 per cent' discount rates. Brands include names such as Indian Terrain, Spykar, Dockers and Park Avenue; and guess what... it only gets better with its sale periods in June, July and August.

DAILY 10.30-9

38 Marine Lines
Mumbai 400 020
Ph. 91 22 2205 8827/ 2209 3116

Chembur
Mumbai 400 071
Ph. 91 22 2521 1861

Parel, Mumbai 400 012
Ph. 91 22 2417 3013/ 2413 3280

Vashi, Mumbai 400 703
Ph. 91 22 2789 4904/ 5694

The Oak Tree

Rs 300 - 8,000

Come around the old oak for a trunk-full of hidden booty. This hole-in-the-wall offers unruffled casual styles, for frenzied out-of-the-blue date fixes to clandestine lovers The excitement here surges from flowing kaftans

18 Cusrow Baug,
Colaba Causeway,
Colaba,
Mumbai 400 005
Ph. 91 22 2281 9031
MAP2 148

and cut-work trousers to crochet bikinis and leaf-print sarongs. Strong-stemmed on accessories, this haunt unearths treasuries of handbags and fashion jewellery.

priyaoaktree@yahoo.co.in

DAILY 11-8 (Sun closed)

The SF Jeans Company

Rs 300 - 3,000

Urban-minded and techno-trendy, The San Frisco Jeans Company bridges home quality street wear for the trilennium. The oil-and-grease-look jeans, creased worn-out wears and boyish bottle-cargos make for fast and furious nights; while mid to ultra-low waists in all levels of flares, invite the babes for a joyride. Shirts, caps and belts gear into the company's products profile too; all fuelling this denim-pump, for a hot and happening vroom!

2 Skyzone,
Phoenix Mills
462 Senapati Bapat Marg
Mumbai 400 013
Ph. 91 22 5666 9129

www.sfjeans.com

MON-FRI 11-9, SAT-SUN 11-9.30

Tiptop Point

Rs 60 - 20,000

When someone recreates a bangle set for the famous K3G mela scene, it has to be the tip of the top. This internet-savvy jewellery store prides itself in having the most diverse selection of bangles in its neighbourhood. Bridal sets completed with maangtikas and paayals, can be personalized to the very shade of your whims here; while bindis, tattoos and Punjabi kaliras can tint any occasion prismatically.

136 VP Road
Sikka Nagar
Mumbai 400 004
Ph. 91 22 2381 0666/ 2382 4793, MAP2 149

tiptopindia@vsnl.com
www.tiptopindia.com

DAILY 10.30-8 (Sun closed)

Tirawa

Rs 295 - 3,000

From trashy to funky – tattered tops, frayed skirts, and faux leather boots –it is all here. From gunji shirts to spiked wristcuffs, this loaded store is a treasure trove for the garage rockers. Other scrap here includes college-wear slingbags, with outlandish motifs for young and hip patrons. Best described as junk-punk, beware, more than a couple of buys could send you on a funk overdrive.

213 Panchsheel Apts
30th Waterfield Road Junction
Bandra (W)
Mumbai 400 050
Ph. 91 22 2642 2404

level1cc@yahoo.com

DAILY 11.30-9.30

Tommy Hilfiger

Prices on Request

Colour your wardrobe in true American spirit as Tommy elevates everyday style with a combination of downtown flair and preppy chic. The saturated red-blue-and-white classic sports and casual wear here get unexpected twists with bold graphics, one-off details and innovative hardware; while the bags, eye and footwear take on a retro look with psychedelic prints and youthful colour.

www.tommy.com

DAILY 10.30-8.30

Dhanraj Mahal
Apollo Bunder
Near Tendulkar's
Mumbai 400 001
Ph. 91 22 5655 0377
MAP2 150

Tonyland

Rs 500 - 15,000

A one-off shop in its neighbourhood, Tonyland offers garments and accessories for every family member. The men's wear section includes shirts and sherwanis, while kids can look cute in Ruff and Gini & Jony clothes. A basic ladies' wear section here, makes this 'land' a convenient stop for locals from the area.

mail@etonyland.com

DAILY 9-9 (Mon closed)

Station Road,
Chembur,
Mumbai 400 071
Ph. 91 22 2529 3490
MAP1 151

Trends

Rs 495 - 3000

Specializing in women's footwear, this store has well-heeled shoes with an emphasis on comfort. The stilettos on offer look vibrant in their multicolours, while funky boots stand tall in varied designs. The majority of the sandals however, aspire to heel above the clichéd shoe-trends in the area.

DAILY 10.30-9 (Sun closed)

Shop No. 3-A
Chinoy Mansion
Warden Road
Mumbai 400 036
Ph. 91 22 2363 1874

Trésorie

Rs 150 onwards

Chime into a world of jewel-studded frames, designer furniture and perfumed candles. Decorative showpieces and mosaic-fringed mirrors at reasonable prices make the treasures here. A two-storey showroom with charming home treasures, this shop offers a fairly tempting priced loot of home accessories.

DAILY 11-8 (Sun closed)

60 A Linking Road
Santacruz (W)
Mumbai 400 054
Ph. 91 22 2660 0243
MAP1 152

Trigger

Rs 595 - 995

An acceptable Indian alternative to international jean companies, Trigger shoots a collection of steadfast products. With a special emphasis on quality fabrics, the jeans predominate in blacks and blues, while earthy beiges and blood reds fire cotton trousers. Tops and denim jackets row up in neat piles here; all waiting to be the targets of your next shopping-hunt.

R Mall, Ground Floor
Shop No. 1, L.B.S. Marg
Mulund (W)
Mumbai 400 080
Ph. 91 22 5599 7966

DAILY 11-10

Trouser Town

Rs 795-2,500

No surprises here, this store specializes in trousers, along with other corporate wear. Stocking Louise Philippe, Van Heusen and Allen Solly in sizes varying from waist 28 to 50, the products here mean serious business. With speedy 15-minute alteration services; it is no wonder that the satisfied citizens of Trouser Town, keep returning for more.

141 M.G. Road
Kala Ghoda, Fort
Mumbai 400 023
Ph. 91 22 2267 2852 / 2906, MAP2 153

vpp28@yahoo.com

DAILY 10.30-8.30 (Sun closed)

Tulsi

Rs 495 - 7,000

The weaves and vivid colours of Tulsi are refreshing amidst the haute couture of The Courtyard. Prodigy of Delhi-based designer Neeru Kumar, this store has indo-westerns, saris, and shawls that offer simple and affordable style to contemporary women. Home furnishings and zardozi batwas, criss-crossed in rural India, are some of the other dreams woven at this shop.

Courtyard
Unit 6, S.P. Centre
41/44 Minoo Desai
Marg, Colaba
Mumbai 400 005
Ph. 91 22 5638 5470/71

tal@satyam.net.in

DAILY 10.30-7.30 (Sun closed)

Turquoise

Rs 750 - 3,000

The designers here strongly believe that women of all sizes should have clothes to compliment their silhouettes. Crafted in natural fabrics, the garbs here mosaic style with comfort; making structured summer kurtis, bejewelled denim tunics and flowing asymmetric skirts in all sizes. Designed classically, the shop's coutures, romance all their beauties in Turquoise hues.

Shellys Estate
Apollo Bundar
Colaba, Opp. Radio Club
Mumbai 400 039
Ph. 91 22 2285 5649

DAILY 10.30-7.30 (Sun closed)

✹ Tuscan Verve

Rs 795 - 1,900

Bail yourself out of a long day with some lounge bohemia. Energizing hunky wardrobes with faux leather shirts and crystal sprinkled zip ups, this studio-like store flashes ooh-la-la styles. Linen kurtis with paisley prints and slouching draw-string pants in cool colours, breeze in for some gushing admiration, while pastel knits bask leisurely on the Tuscan racks. For a spiffy look at chilled out prices, stop by this Verve-ed store and make those powder puffed girls swoon...

DAILY 11.30-10

Linking Road, Khar
Mumbai 400 052
Ph. 91 22 26468 422/ 0385, **MAP1 154**

Uni Style Image

Rs 300 - 800

Not making any unique style statements, Uni Style Image emphasizes on bright and simply designed monotone shirts for men and women. Casual and comfortable is the catch phrase of the clothing quotient here, while the rest of the daily-wear bottoms and sweatshirts invite you in as you pass by.

mumbai@unistyleimage.com
www.unistyleimage.com

DAILY 11.30-10

103 Heera Panna
Shopping Centre, Haji Ali
Mumbai 400 026
248 Linking Road
Opp. National College
Bandra (W)
Mumbai 400 050
Ph. 91 22 2640 9063/ 2642 1127

United Colors of Benetton

Rs 299 - 5,400

Straight-forward and cross-cultured, this Italian brand continues to be a reliable source of well-made knitwear in a brilliant palette of solid colours. Dresses, pants and lingerie are the staples of the women's collections here, while men can choose from hooded sweatshirts, checked shirts, and pin-striped trousers. With its funky laptop cases and tinted eyewear, UCB is all set to multicolour your day.

DAILY 10.30-9

U-37, 38 & 39, InOrbit Mall, Link Road
Malad (W), Mumbai 400 064

Kanchenjunga Building
Cumballa Hill
Mumbai 400 026
Ph. 91 22 2387 1450 / 1451, **MAP2 155**

38, Raheem Mansion
Colaba Causeway
Mumbai 400 05

Crossroads, C-101 - 103
1/F, 28 Pt. M.M. Malviya
Road, Haji Ali
Mumbai 400 024

Raheja Chamber, Linking
Road, Santacruz (W)
Mumbai 400 049

Urban Wear

Rs 1,500 onwards

Amidst export surplus and seconds stores in the WTC, this urban boutique is a refreshing respite. Sanguine salwar kameezes with rich embroideries beckon the more conventional types, while fluid side tie-ups with floral designs blow away the frivolous kinds. For an uptown lunch or a backyard bash, ladies, swan

1st Floor,
World Trade Centre,
Cuffe Parade,
Mumbai 400 005

into this couture house to wade all of your options.

Urvashi

Rs 275-50,000

Another rank to add to the scores of abounding sari shops in its neighbourhood, Urvashi also offers 'exclusive' lehengas and dress materials. Specializing in traditional drapes, regional saris from across the state borders roll their way in here, while modern designs and threads cascade with pride. For a sea of nymphy products at watered-down prices, trickle in.

Marine Lines
Mumbai 400 002

Urvee's

Rs 400 - 35,000

Aromatic essences, clothes, and art blend smoothly together at this aspiring shop. Diamante-studded saris and sequinned lehengas are perfectly harmonized with beaded handbags and sandals; while Jain clients are serviced with outfits exclusively made of synthetic fabrics. Orders on pure fabrics and sherwanis for men are accepted here too.

urvee2410@yahoo.com

DAILY 10-8.30 (Sun closed)

G-3 Mini Sudarshan
Building
22 LD Ruparel Marg
Malabar Hill
Mumbai 400 006
Ph. 91 22 2368 4069

Vaishali

Rs 10 - 1,000

Look out for tinselled names of the glam-world who reportedly visit this shop. Wooden, acrylic and lac bangles with innumerous embellishments jingle here, while personalized crystal name bangles clink to be noticed. Custom-made bindis spot in too; making sure that you dot your look just right.

DAILY 10-7 (Sun closed)

Chandralok 'A'
97 Napean Sea Road
Mumbai 400 026
Ph. 91 22 2367 8534
MAP1 156

Vaishali

Rs 1,000 - 80,000

A big and buzzing sari chain, Vaishali won't win any design accolades but has tons of variety on hand at fair prices. After 30 years of business, the store's in-house embroidered saris stand out in their drapes, while the provincial ones coyly shadow behind. The selections are easy to browse through, organized by style and lauded by keen salesmen – all conducive to hassle-free shopping.

DAILY 10.30-8.30 (Sun closed)

91 Shalimar Building
Marine Drive (W)
Mumbai 400 002
Ph. 91 22 2281 8298
MAP2 157

10 Vaishali Shopping
Centre, JVPD Scheme
Juhu, Mumbai 400 049
Ph. 91 22 5693 4926

11 Subh Laxmi
Shopping Centre
Poddar Road, Malad (E),
Mumbai 400 064
Ph. 91 22 2880 6225

Vāmā

Rs 130 onwards

From Dior watches and Oakley eyewear to Levi's jeans and Nike tracks, Vāmā makes way for premium luxury brands in its upmarket showroom. Housing various lines from casual to bridal wear, this multi-dimensional store cuts into the trend cross-section of every market. J.J. Vallaya and Manju & Bobby Grover also strike their presence here, while other high profile designers such as Kimono and Suneet Varma charm customers with ease.

Kanchenjunga,
72 Peddar Road,
Mumbai 400 026
Ph. 91 22 23871450
MAP2 158

DAILY 10.30-9

Vandana Creation

Rs 3,000 - 40,000

An offspring of its fabric retailing section, Vandana offers a diverse range of saris, salwar kameezes and lehengas. In-house designer creations in pure and mix fabrics are embellished with metallic threads and spangles here; while an exclusive inner section is graced with heavy bridal lehengas and snooty cocktail saris.

vandanafabrics@vsnl.net

Shop 10, Chandralok 'A'
97 Napean Sea Road,
Mumbai 400 006
Ph. 91 22 2368 0527/
2368 3637, MAP2 159

DAILY 10-8 (Sun closed)

Vanzasons

Rs 1,400 - 10,000

Synonymous with bandhani shopping, Vanzasons is a popular name with Mumbai ladies. Unveiling products exclusively from Jamnagar, this shop has saris to strut on every occasion–from bridal mehendis to casual luncheons. Although shopping here might feel like searching for a needle in a haystack at times; be patient, you will be rewarded!

106 Marine Mansion
1st Marine Street
Near Dhobi Talao Masjid
Mumbai 400 002
Ph. 91 22 2203 9772/
2205 9799, MAP2 160

DAILY 10-7 (Sun closed)

Vareli

Rs 250 - 1,050

Garden's more glamorous twin, Vareli hoards popular merchandise including saris featured so elegantly in the advertisements. Comfortable cotton drapes with garden prints borrow in spirit from its sibling, while linens trimmed with jute look nonchalant in their geometrical motifs. With reasonable prices, Vareli calls out to the young at heart.

Shop No. 3
Mahalaxmi Chambers
23 Bhulabhai Desai Road
Mumbai 400 026
Ph. 91 22 2351 4554

Garden Bargain Centre
(Second's Shop)
45 A Panchratna
Mama Parmanand Marg
Opera House
Mumbai 400 007
Ph. 91 22 2368 6328

DAILY 10.30-7.30 (Sun closed)

Vastra Kosh

Rs 3,000 - 8,000

If you are looking for an Indian outfit in bucolic tones within a mid-high budget, this tiny store is worth a peek. Beaded kurtis in natural fibres, teamed with earthy coloured raw silk trousers swing modestly on their racks, while restrained shawls shy away in the background. Largely targetting middle-aged ladies, this 'vastra' cache has much to offer.

vak@satyam.net.in

DAILY 10-8

Shop No. 224
Crossroads
28, Pt. M.M. Malviya Rd
Haji Ali
Mumbai 400 034
Ph. 91 22 2352 1126

Venilal Saris/ Venilal's

Rs 2,000 - 30,000

You are what you wear; and here at Venilal Saris, you can be assured of being well-bred. Frivolous romantic ruffles whisper sweet nothings here, while ornate bridal saris tell a tale of a 100-year-old epoch. Saris to match every hue of India's rich heritage, Venilal's collections assure its customers a cultured buy.

dvenilal@vsnl.com (Morvi Lane)
venilals@vsnl.com (Dr. Atmaram Marchant Road)

DAILY 11-8 (Sun closed)

Shop No. 2 A/B
Stone Building
Morvi Lane
Off Chowpatty Seaface
Mumbai 400 007
Ph. 91 22 2368 0160/
2368 0161, **MAP2 161**

Venilal's Estate, 34
Dr. Atmaram Merchant
Road, Bhuleshwar
Mumbai 400 002
Ph. 91 22 2208 515

Vikram Phadnis

Rs 3,000 onwards

Swerve in for some high-octave Bollywood dhamaaka. Spanish-inspired interiors toast cocktail numbers and trousseau toffees here, while kimono tops with cigarette bottoms cheer the casual wine-luncheons. Indo-westerns and lehengas sizzle the Urmila Matondkar dances, whereas hunky jackets and kurtis swoon over Salman Khan chests. Fashion full throttle, Bollywood style, Vikram Phadnis tinsel-tints the front-row gliterrati.

vikramphadnis@hotmail.com
www.vikramphadnis.com

DAILY 11-8 (Sun closed)

Navratan
AB Nair Road, Opp. Rain
Juhu, Mumbai 400 049
Ph. 91 22 3096 1528 /
1529, **MAP1 162**

Vividha

Rs 20 - 250

It is almost like trying to spot the number of stars in the sky; the bindis here will dazzle your eyes. With over 1000 designs to choose from, you can find bindis in every avatar, from the kum-kum powder ones to the stick-on variety. With added frills of bangles and bracelets, be assured of dotting the latest trends.

DAILY 10-8 (Sun closed)

23 Chandralok 'A',
97 Napean Sea Road,
Mumbai 400 026
Ph. 91 22 2369 6185
MAP2 163

Vogad's

Rs 500 - 10,000

This upmarket store is a bit of a misfit in its low-key neighbourhood. Flaunting acclaimed brands such as Van Heusen and Zodiac, Vogad's is all set to dress the corporate world, with a hint of relaxed style. Also spiriting the ethnic end, this well-stacked shop surges a selection of sherwanis and jodhpuris; all at level-headed prices.

TUE-SUN 9.30-9.30

Siddharth House
Plot No. 11 A
19th Road, Chembur
Mumbai 400 071
Ph. 91 22 2527 7455/56

W

Rs 300 onwards

A simple letter for the contemporary woman, W, provides modest and trendy clothing for regular office wear. Focusing on fusion work, the shop couples pants with kurtis, and sprays the outfits with a flush of chromatic dupattas. Made of 100 per cent cotton, the products here allow women to mix and match their outfits to suit their own styles.

milestone1@hathway.com

MON-FRI 11-9.30, SAT-SUN 11-10

F-4, InOrbit Mall
New Link Road
Malad (W)
Mumbai 400 064
Ph. 91 22 5643 2985/
3259 5059

Cusrow Baug,
Colaba
Mumbai 400 005

Warp 'n' Weft

Rs 800 - 40,000

Stretching across the shop, olive green walls and wooden interiors weave elegance into this shop. Banarsi saris, with real zari work and brocade rule the rolls here, while jacquard fabrics, kota block-prints, and kora dupattas, make their presence felt. Lehengas and salwars can also be stitched-by-order.

MON-FRI 10.30-7.30

Sethna Building
55 Maharshi Karve Road
Marine Lines
Mumbai 400 002
Ph. 91 22 22000554
MAP2 164

Weekender

Rs 85 - 1,095

A peppy stop on a weekend off, this shop offers casual clothing for all. Cotton trousers, short skirts and basic tees come in their basic sensibilities here, while prices follow the same theme. The shop's kiddie range of 'Toon-World' products is especially cute, with cartoon prints and colourful hats; sprucing up the naughtiest of wardrobes.

DAILY 10.30-9.30

No. 3, Prerna Co.Housing Society, Flat No.67, Lokhandwala, Andheri (W), Mumbai 400 053
Ph. 91 22 2632 2951

Runwall Mall, Mulund (W), Mumbai 400 080

Unit No. 2
Ground Floor, Building C
Cross Roads
28, Pt. M.M. Malviya Road
Haji Ali M-34
Mumbai 400 026
Ph. 91 22 2351 5083

711 Bharat Bhavan
Linking Road
Bandra
Mumbai 400 052
Ph. 91 22 2605 8225
MAP1 165

Unit No. 10, Skyzone, Phoenix Mills Lower Parel,
Senapati Bapat Marg, M-13, Mumbai 400 013
Ph. 91 22 5660 1048

Vashi Centre 1,
Mumbai 400 703
Ph. 91 22 2781 2237

Westside

Rs 50 onwards

Follow your compass here to find reasonable products for every age. Indian outfits in khadi fabrics and western apparels for women, stand out in their simplicity, while suave shirts take over the men's business wear section. Children can frolic in a variety of irressistable chirpy clothes at their disposal here; while the shopping-day-out can have a delicious end with a cookie and a cuppa chai at the in-store café.

westside15@trent-tata.com
westside11@trent-tata.com
westside4@trent-tata.com

DAILY 11-9

R-Mall
L.B.S Marg
Mulund (West)
Mumbai 400080
Ph. 91 22 5555 4281/82

Army and Navy Buildibg
Ground floor, Kala
Ghoda, 148, Mahatma
Gandhi Road,
Mumbai 400 001
Ph. 91 22 5636 0500

39, N S Patkar Marg,
Mumbai – 400 012
Ph. 91 22 2384 1729/
1730, MAP2 166

What?

Rs 600 - 10,000

From slinky-slim dresses to jazzy shirts, this shop has everything for the dancing diva and her male escort. Popular for its spin-off clothes and bonny handbags, the store also enthuses ethnic outfits for women and formal suits for men in its collections. So the next time you are asked for a reasonably priced store to shop at; answer the question with a 'What?'

what_mumbai@yahoo.com

DAILY 10-10.30

8 Juhu Tara Road
Opp L.W. Marriott
Mumbai 400 049
Ph. 91 22 5693 0773/
5693 0773

What's Pink

Rs 500 - 3,500

Fashion goes head to toe with this cherry shop that blushes with the colour pink. Dolled with beaded curtains, this recess treasures corsets, pants and slings – all kitschily funked up with embroidery and sequins work – for women; while men can indulge in smart footwear. What's Pink is a pretty and peppy source for enthusiastic teeny boppers, who can never have too much pizzaz.

DAILY 11.30-8 (Sun closed)

A.N. House
Shop No. 2
31st Road
Lane Opp. Shoppers'
Stop
Bandra (W)
Mumbai 400 050
Ph. 91 22 2645 8875

White Window

Rs 500 Ownards

Twinkle Khanna's suburban showroom windows a classy collection of home décor accessories, from silverware and art glassware to her mother, Dimple Kapadia's,

Lokhandwala Complex
Andheri
Mumbai 400 003
Ph. 91 22 5675 0367
MAP1 167

designer candles. Juxtaposing the antique with the modern and mixing opulence with contemporary, Tania Deol's ornate furniture stand out here, displayed amongst the art works of Sunil Padwal and Anjolie Ela Mennon.

DAILY 11-8 (Sun closed)

Wills Lifestyle

Rs 295 - 8,000

Practically cut and classically designed, the products here will a 'proper' lifestyle. Stacked in neat piles, the brand's casual collection in understated colours, invites you to Sunday brunches, whiles the formal range chauffeurs you on fancy night-outs. Furla handbags and Valentino sunglasses hint an international flavour, to this otherwise Indian Lifestyle shop.

DAILY 10.30-9.30

InOrbit Mall, Linking Road, Malad (W), Mumbai 400 064
Ph. 91 22 5643 0497/ 5643 0499

No. 6 & 6A
Tirupati Apartments
Bhulabhai Desai Road
Warden Road
Mumbai 400 026
Ph. 91 22 2492 6210/ 2492 6074

23 & 32
Ruki Mahal
Co-op Housing Society
Colaba Causeway
Mumbai 400 005
Ph. 91 22 2281 8261/ 2281 8325

Woodland

Rs 45 - 4,000

An established brand, Woodland is hailed for its weatherproof shoes. The brand's leather mocassins and floaters also promise to serve their masters well, while the 'camels' range is especially light weight and heat repellant. Also on offer are sturdy windcheaters.

DAILY 10-9

Choice Centre, 24 Ramdas Naik Marg, Hill Road
Bandra (W), Mumbai 400 050

Plot No. 535
Shop No. 3
Nav Meghdoot Co-op
Housing Society Ltd.
Linking Road, Khar (W)
Mumbai 400 052
Ph. 91 22 2646 3902

York House, SBS Road
Opp. Electric House
Colaba Causeway
Mumbai 400 001
MAP2 168

Wrangler

Rs 395 - 1,500

Equipping babes and hunks with the rough and tough look, Wrangler jeans are made of good quality materials that don't tear easily. The brand's 'fashion jeans', include sandblasts, fades, and crinkles, while the casual collection is more straightforward with solid colours and stripes. Formal trousers complete this contemporary store with their unwrangled and refined moods.

DAILY 10.30-8.30

70 Empire Mahal, Dadar (E)
Mumbai 400 014
Ph. 91 22 2416 6235

Shop No. 22/ A, Kushrow Building
Shahid Bhagat Singh Rd, Colaba Causeway
Mumbai 400 005
Ph. 91 22 2284 0722/ 5636 8987

Skyzone Mall
Phoenix Mills
462 Senapati Bapat Marg,
Lower Parel
Mumbai 400 013
Ph. 91 22 5662 3070

X'Mex Clothing

Rs 295-1,500

Providing clothes for Generation X, X'Mex imports style straight from the Far East. Denim frilled skirts, drawstring pants, and sporty footwear whisp their way in here, while ruched zipper t-shirts and camouflage bottoms zoom right out. A footloose store with prices to match; you can finally 'Do, what you wanna do here.'

DAILY 12.15-9.15

24/35 G. Floor, Citimall, Adjacent to Fame Adlabs, New Link Road, Andheri (W)
Mumbai 400 053
Ph. 91 22 5692 0037

1, Kamal Apartments
Lokhandwala Complex
Andheri (W)
Mumbai 400 053
Ph. 91 22 2630 2542

Yamini

Rs 150 onwards

Designer linen, tablecloths, bolsters, curtains, napkins, and even lampshades are available in this store, which has become a favourite with Mumbai ladies. Reva Sethi, the fashion designer responsible for the collection here is adept at combining materials to create fascinating new textures. And what's more, you can even consult her to design new fabrics for your home.

DAILY 10.30-7.30

President House
Wodehouse Rd, Colaba
Mumbai 400 005
Ph. 91 22 2218 4143/45
MAP2 169

34 Turner Road
Patkars Bungalow
Bandra (W)
Mumbai 400 050
Ph. 91 22 2643 7667

Yantra

Prices on Request

This plush flagship store of Birla Lifestyle houses works of over 22 designers. Boasting of world-renowned brands like B&B, Cappellini, Fendi and Kartell, along with an impressive string of Indian names such as Priti Paul, Yogesh Jaikishan and Abraham & Thakore, this store is one of its kind. Exhibited here is upholstered, woven sea grass, bent glass, polypropylene plastic, leather and outdoor furniture; while the table accessories and crockery here promise to furnish your space in style.

TUE-SUN 11-7

Queen's Mansion
Prescott Road
Fort, Mumbai 400 001
Ph. 91 22 2200 3621/22/23, MAP2 170

77 Napean Sea Road
Opp Dariya Mahal
Mumbai 400 006
Ph. 91 22 2369 3820 / 2362 22445

You

Rs 150 - Rs 4,000

Think You can't get any funkier? Think again. Floral dresses, sequinned tubes and bright pants, gypsy up the racks here, while jewellery, scarves and handbags complete the nomadic look. With offbeat designs, riveting contrasts and added frills, the caravan of products here assures its customers a colourful joy ride.

DAILY 10.30-7 (Sun closed)

2 Cornelian,
Kemps Corner
104, August Kranti Marg
Mumbai 400 036
Ph. 91 22 2382 6972/73
MAP2 171

Zedds

Rs 1,250 - 10,000

A small shop with a plethora of Indian semi-formals, Zedds has streaks to match every hue of the sky. Creating clothes with unpredictable twists, the designer here teams salwar kurtas with cut work pants, and mermaid lehengas with noodle tops. Perfectly fused with tradition and trend, the shop's outfits are made for cocktail party compliments.

jzedds@vsnl.net

DAILY 10-8 (Sun closed)

3 Shernaz Building
Juhu Tara Road
Next to JW Marriot Hotel
Mumbai 400 009
Ph. 91 22 2612 4871/ 2613 3788
Mob. 91 98200 48635

Zinc

Rs 75 onwards

If you want to make a style leap to cheap-chic, this store will be your junk-haven. A complete make-over collection ranges from club wear and footwork to swimwear and lingerie. The store's true platinum however lies in its special corner devoted to rusty jewellery and waist belts. Locally lauded as an unmined metal, this shop could zing up any wardrobe.

meetukumar@hotmail.com

B-2 Gagangiri Co-op. Society
Carter Road
Khar Danda
Mumbai 400 052
Ph. 91 22 2604 8807

Zodiac

Rs 799 - 3,000

This international brand offers classic office shirts in a choice of single and double cuffs. Providing sleek trousers in chinos and linens as well, the bottoms here are made of wrinkle-free fabrics for greater ease and comfort. Office style accessories such as cuff links and tiepins embellish the corporate appearance, while the more fashionable collection, Zod! appeals to the young shopper.

DAILY 10-8

A.N. House, Shop No.3, 31st Road,
Opp. Shoppers' Stop
Bandra (W), Mumbai 400 050
Ph. 91 22 2642 9333

Kalaghoda, Opp. Mumbai University,
Mumbai 400 001
Ph. 91 22 2267 3723

Om Rameshwar, Opp. Samarth Bhandar, Thane
Mumbai 400 601
Ph. 91 22 2642 9333

Crawford Market
Opp. GT Hospital
Mumbai 400 003
Ph. 91 22 2206 0014

The Taj Mahal Hotel
Apollo Bunder
Mumbai 400 001
Ph. 91 22 2202 6211

Hotel Oberoi
Nariman Point
Mumbai 400 021
Ph. 91 22 2282 1991

CR2, Nariman Point
Mumbai 400 021

Matru Ashish
Napean Sea Road
Mumbai 400 006
Ph. 91 22 2368 1729
MAP2 172

Grand Hyatt Plaza
Santacruz (E),
Mumbai 400 055
Ph. 91 22 5676/1234
Daily 11-9

Zooni

Rs 895 - 16,000

This graceful store has clothing for conservative women with larger silhouettes.

4 Breach Candy
Art Gallery,
63-A
Breach Candy

Clean cuts and understated colours dominate the style here, while products range from cotton and voile shirts to long skirts and drawstring trousers. Embellished with minimal sequin and gara work, the shop's attires can also be bought online and delivered to your doorstep.

Mumbai 400 026
Ph. 91 22 2369 3254
MAP2 173

10 Mangal Darshan
Waterfield Road
Bandra (W)
Mumbai 400 050
Ph. 91 22 2643 2493

info@zooni.net
www.zooni.net

DAILY 10-9 (Sun closed)

4 2 14 Originals

Rs 199 - 599

Spring has sprung at this store that stocks western clothing for children. Supplying colourful clothes ranging from Spider Man print t-shirts and dungarees for boys to flowery spaghetti tops and whiskered jeans for girls, the shop sells good quality products at fair prices. A small range of undergarments along with hair clips, belts and socks are available here as well; all to make your naughty devils look endearingly angelic.

Shop No. 13, Basera
Lokhandwala Complex
Andheri (W)
Mumbai 400 058
Ph. 91 22 5692 3427

Centre One Mall
Shop No. 14
Sector 30-A, Vashi
Navi Mumbai 400 705
Ph. 91 22 2781 2046

DAILY 11-9

7 BEST Marg

Rs 1,000 onwards

This fashion address houses the collections of four eminent Indian designers. Kavita Bhartia combines Indian designs with international trends in her couture, while Ogaan includes exquisite Indian and western clothing and accessories for formal occasions. The third designer, Ranna Gill, derives inspiration from folk costumes and displays a playful and classy line of ethnic clothing; while Cue and H2O – Rohit Gandhi and Rahul Khanna – combine comfort and style, especially in their men's formal ensembles.

Vaswani House
1st Floor, 7 Best Marg
Colaba
Mumbai 400 005
Ph. 91 22 2285 6559
MAP2 1

ogaan@mantraonline.com
rannagill@hotmail.com

DAILY 11-8 (Sun closed)

SHOP-WISE INDEX

SHOP WISE INDEX

CHILDREN'S & INFANT WEAR

DEPARTMENTAL STORES

LIFESTYLE STORES

FOR MEN

ACTIVE WEAR

United Colors of Benetton
Wills Lifestyle
Woodland

CASUAL - INDIAN

Anokhi
Be
Cambridge
Charagh Din
Cottons
Cottons (Jaipur)
Culture Shop
Fabindia
Finlay's
H. Couture
Kala Niketan
Kaysons
Libas
Men's Boulevard
Neeta Lulla
Pramanik
Pratap
Ravissant
Roman Park
Roopam
Sheetal
Sheetal Design Studio
Shringar
Studio F
Studio Sajid
Telon
The Double Bull Wagon
Tonyland
Vogad's

CASUAL - WESTERN

Abraham & Thakore
Adidas
Allen Solly
Apparel Store
Arrow
Barefoot
Be
Blackberrys
Body Sport
Cambridge
Candy
Charagh Din
Clothes Rack
Color Plus
Cottons (Jaipur)
Cotton Lollypop
Cotton World Corp
Cottons
Culture Shop
Daks
Dockers
Energy
Ermenegildo Zegna
Fabindia
Fila & Proline
Finlay's
Fuel
Gabbana
H. Couture
Hangten
High
Hugo Boss
Hum India
Indigo Nation
Instyle
Ixtapa
J'aime
Just Carnival
Kink
Lacoste
Lawman
Lee
Levi's
Live-in Store
Lord & Taylor
Louise Philippe
Man O' Man
Marco Ricci
Marks & Spencer
Men's Boulevard
MTV Factory Outlet
Nagma's
Neeta Lulla
Nike
Nimesis
Oobe
Originals Unlimited!
Peacock Forever
Pepe
Phat Fish
Planet Fashion
Planet Sports
Potion 9
Pramanik
Pratap
Provogue
Provogue Lounge
Ragz Genes
Rainbow
Raymond's
Reebok
Reid & Taylor
Rock Fashion Studio
Rockport
Selection Centre
Sheetal
Sheetal Design Studio
Si Branché
Spykar Jeans
Tango
Tent
The Double Bull Wagon
The Loot
The SF Jeans Company
Tirawa
Tommy Hilfiger
Tonyland
Trigger
Trouser Town
Tuscan Verve
Uni Style Image
United Colors of Benetton
Vogad's
Weekender
What?
Wills Lifestyle
Woodland
Wrangler
X'Mex Clothing
Zodiac

CLUB WEAR

Ashish N Soni
Boulevard Benzer/ Rocky S Jeans
Color Plus
Designs Unlimited
Gabbana
High
Instyle
Ixtapa
J'aime
Just Carnival
Kimaya
Kink
Nagma's
Narendra Kumar
Offbeat
Oz
Phat Fish
Potion 9
Provogue Lounge
Rainbow
Reid & Taylor
Rock Fashion Studio
Rock S Jeans
Salim Asgarally
Si Branché
Sign O' Times
Telon
Tirawa
Tuscan Verve
What?
Zodiac

EXECUTIVE WEAR

Allen Solly
Arrow
Ashish N Soni

Babubhai Bhavanji
Blackberrys
Burlingtons of Bombay
Canali
Charagh Din
Color Plus
Cottons
Daks
Dockers
Enamour
Ermenegildo Zegna
Finlay's
Gabbana
High Street
Hugo Boss
Indigo Nation
Instyle
Just Carnival
Kachins Clothing
Lacoste
Lord & Taylor
Louise Philippe
Man O' Man
Marco
Marks & Spencer
Men's Boulevard
Millionaire
Ofran
Originals Unlimited!
Planet Fashion
Pramanik
Provogue
Provogue Lounge
Rahul Agasti
Raymond's
Reid & Taylor
Roman Park
Si Branché
The Double Bull Wagon
Tonyland
Trouser Town
United Colors of Benetton
Vogad's
Wills Lifestyle
Zodiac

FORMAL - INDIAN

Abu Jani & Sandeep Khosla
Adarsh Gill
Amber and Shirrin
Arjun Khanna
Babubhai Bhavanji
Benu Sehgall Originals
Burlingtons of Bombay
Charagh Din
Designer Studio
Designs Unlimited
Enamour
Ensemble
Fabindia
Fuel
Gabbana
High Street
Instyle
James Ferriera
Just Carnival
Kachins Clothing
Kala Niketan
Krishna Mehta
Libas
Marco
Mélange
Men's Boulevard
Millionaire
Neeta Lulla
Offbeat
Pramanik
Pratap
Priya & Chintan
Rahul Agasti
Ravissant
Ritu Kumar
Rohit Bal
Roopam
Sajid Design Studio
Salim Asgarally
Sheetal
Sheetal Design Studio
Shlok
Shringar
Studio Sinitta
Sushobhit
Tarun Tahiliani
Telon
The Double Bull Wagon
Tonyland
Urvee's
Vikram Phadnis

FORMAL - WESTERN

Abraham & Thakore
Allen Solly
Amber and Shirrin
Ananya
Arjun Khanna
Ashish N Soni
Babubhai Bhavanji
Be:
Blackberrys
Boulevard Benzer/ Rocky S Jeans
Burlingtons of Bombay
Canali
Charagh Din
Color Plus
Daks
Designs Unlimited
Enamour
Ermenegildo Zegna
Gabbana
H. Couture
High Street
Hugo Boss
Indigo Nation
Instyle
Ishna
Ixtapa
James Ferriera
Just Carnival
Kachins Clothing
Lacoste
Libas
Lord & Taylor
Louise Philippe
Man O' Man
Marco
Marks & Spencer
Men's Boulevard
Millionaire
Narendra Kumar
Offbeat
Peacock Forever
Planet Fashion
Pramanik
Pratap
Provogue
Provogue Lounge
Rahul Agasti
Raymond's
Reebok
Reid & Taylor
Rohit Bal
Roman Park
Roopam
Sajid Design Studio
Salim Asgarally
Sheetal
Sheetal Design Studio
Shlok
Shringar
Studio Sinitta
The Double Bull Wagon
Tonyland
Trouser Town
Tuscan Verve
Vikram Phadnis
Vogad's
What?
Wills Lifestyle
Zodiac
7 BEST Marg

INNER & NIGHTWEAR

Color Plus
Finlay's
Gabbana

Hum India
Instyle
Just Carnival
Lacoste
Man O' Man
Marks & Spencer
Planet Fashion
Roman Park
SD Lounge
Sheetal
Sleep-ins
Tommy Hilfiger
Tonyland
United Colors of Benetton
Vogad's
Roman Park
Royal Leather
Samsonite
Satya Paul
Scandal
Si Branché
Sign O' Times
Sun - Way Leather House
Tommy Hilfiger
Uni Style Image
United Colors of Benetton
Vogad's
What?
Wills Lifestyle
Zodiac

LEATHER GOODS & ACCESSORIES

Adidas
Aigner
Aldo
Bally
Bata
Cambridge
Cheemo
Christina
Color Plus
Culture Shop
Ego
Gabbana
Hidesign
Hugo Boss
Images
Instyle
Jewelart
Joy Shoes
Lacoste
Leather Farm
Leather Touch
Louise Philippe
Louis Vuitton
Marco
Marco Ricci
Marks & Spencer
Metro
Mont Blanc
Nike
Pepe
Planet Sports
Provogue
Provogue Lounge
Rahul Agasti
Rasulbhai Adamji
Raymond's
Reebok
Regal
Rock Fashion Studio
Rockport
Roma

LOUNGE WEAR

Amber and Shirrin
Ashish N Soni
Barefoot
Be:
Blackberrys
Boulevard Benzer/ Rocky S Jeans
Charagh Din
Designs Unlimited
Fuel
Gabbana
H. Couture
Hugo Boss
J'aime
Kimaya
Kink
Krishna Mehta
Marco Ricci
Narendra Kumar
Offbeat
Orange Plum
Peacock Forever
Potion 9
Phat Fish
Provogue
Rainbow
Rohit Bal
Salim Asgarally
Sheetal
Sheetal Design Studio
Telon
Tent
The SF Jeans Company
Tommy Hilfiger
Tuscan Verve
X'Mex Clothing
Zodiac

SHOES

Abraham & Thakore
Adidas
Aldo
Bally
Barefoot
Bata
Body Sport
Bon Bon
Burlingtons of Bombay
Candy
Caxton Sports
Citywalk
Designs Unlimited
Empire
Faith
Fila & Proline
Footsie
Frenzy
FuToes
H. Couture
Habit Shoes
High
High Street
Hugo Boss
Ixtapa
Joy Shoes
Just Carnival
Lord's
Marco Ricci
Marks & Spencer
Metro
Nike
Part 1 Accessories
Planet Sports
Potion 9
Pratap
Pretty Walk
Provogue
Reebok
Regal
Revolutions
Rock Fashion Studio
Rockport
Scandal
Selection Centre
Shlok
Sign O' Times
Studio M
The Loft
The Loot
Tommy Hilfiger
What?
What's Pink
Woodland

WEDDING WEAR

Abu Jani & Sandeep Khosla
Adarsh Gill
Amber and Shirrin
Arjun Khanna

Benu Sehgall Originals
Boulevard Benzer/ Rocky S Jeans
Burlingtons of Bombay
Canali
Daks
Designer Studio
Ensemble
Ermenegildo Zegna
Gabbana
Hugo Boss
Instyle
James Ferriera
Just Carnival
Kala Niketan
Libas
Marco
Mélange
Men's Boulevard
Millionaire
Neeta Lulla
Offbeat
Pratap
Priya & Chintan
Purple Kids
Rahul Agasti
Ravissant
Raymond's
Reid & Taylor
Rohit Bal
Sajid Design Studio
Salim Asgarally
Sheetal Design Studio
Shringar
Studio Sinitta
Sushobhit
Tarun Tahiliani
Telon
The Double Bull Wagon
Urvee's
Vikram Phadnis
7 BEST Marg

WINTER WEAR

Babubhai Bhavanji
Clothes Rack
Daks
Ermenegildo Zegna
Hugo Boss
Just Carnival
Man O' Man
Marco
MTV Factory Outlet
Si Branché
Tommy Hilfiger
Uni Style Image
United Colors of Benetton

STREET MARKETS

Bhuleshwar
Colaba Causeway
Fashion Street
Hill Road
Linking Road
Lokhandwala
The Galleria, Powai

FOR WOMEN

ACTIVE WEAR

Adidas
Apparel Store
Body Sport
Charagh Din
Chemistry
Clothes Rack
Cotton World Corp
Eternia
Fila and Proline
Habit Shoes
Hangten
Hum India
JVP
Lacoste
Madame
Mango/ MNG
Nagma's
Nike
Oobe
Oz
Pagli
Part 1 Accessories
Phat Fish
Planet Sports
Pretty Walk
Reebok
Rockport
Selection Centre
Si Branché
Star Sports
The Champion Sports
The Loot
Tommy Hilfiger
United Colors of Benetton
Wills Lifestyle
Woodland
X'Mex Clothing

BINDIS & BANGLES

Aadi's
Abhushan
Beauti Art
DeeJay
Kala Niketan
New Pink Lady
Roop Milan
Tiptop Point
Vaishali
Vividha

BRIDAL & TROUSSEAU

Aadi's
Aari
Abu Jani & Sandeep Khosla
Adarsh Gill
Amber and Shirrin
AND Designs/ Anita Dongre
Antè Body
Archana Kochhar
Arjun Khanna
Azeem Khan
Benu Sehgall Originals
Bhakti Creations
Boulevard Benzer/ Rocky S Jeans
Brahma Selections
Burlingtons of Bombay
Dadar Emporium
De Hauz Khas
Designer Studio
Ensemble
Gold Leaf
Golden Thimble
Hast Kala
Hurley's
India Emporium
Indian States
Ishna
Jaipur Saree Kendra
James Ferriera
Kala Niketan
Kaysons
Kimaya
Krishna Mehta
Lāzāree
Maheka Mirpuri/ IV Fashion Life
Mayuri
Mélange
Milap
Mogra
Naina's
Nalli Sarees
Neeta Lulla
Nisha Sagar
Paaneri
Pagli
Paraphernalia
Passion Flower
Payal Singhal
Pitambari

Private Collections
Priya & Chintan
Puravi Modgil
Rabani & Rakha
Radhika Naik
Raj Kamal Sarees
Rangoli
Ravissant
Reshma
Rink's
Ritu Kumar
Rohit Bal
Roop Milan
Roop Sangam
Roopam
Sagar
Sakhi
Salim Asgarally
Shakun
Sheetal Design Studio
Shlok
Studio Lingerie
Suneet Varma
Sushobhit
Tarun Tahiliani
The Indian Textile Company
Urvee's
Vaishali
Vandana Creation
Vanzasons
Venilal Saris/ Venilal's
Vikram Phadnis
Warp 'n' Weft
7 BEST Marg

CASUAL - INDIAN

Aakanksha
Abraham & Thakore
Adarsh Gill
Amâya
Anokhi
Bandhej
Be:
Bhakti Creations
Biba
Boulevard Benzer/ Rocky S Jeans
Brahma Selections
Candy
Christina
Cottons
Cottons (Jaipur)
Culture Shop
Dadar Emporium
De Hauz Khas
Enamour
Eternia
Fabindia
Finlay's
Garden
Hakoba
Hast Kala
Hurley's
India Emporium
Indian States
Istaa
Istante
Jaipur Bandhej
Jaipur Saree Kendra
Jashn
Kala Niketan
Kaysons
Lāzāree
Malabar Boutique
Mayuri
Mehendi
Mélange
Milap
Mogra
Moksh
Ms. Banjaran
Naina's
Nalli Sarees
Neeta Lulla
On My Own (OMO)
Paaneri
Pagli
Paraphernalia
Peacock Forever
Pitambari
Pramanik
Pratap
Queens Emporium
Rangoli
Ravissant
Rink's
Ritu Kumar
Rohit Bal
Roop Milan
Roop Sangam
Roopam
Rui
Sagar
Sakhi
Satya Paul
Saundarya
Sheetal
Sheetal Design Studio
Shilpa K
Shringar
Shruti
Studio Prêt
Studio Sajid
S'warya
The Double Bull Wagon
Tonyland
Tulsi
Urban Wear
Urvashi
Vaishali
Vandana Creation
Vanzasons
Vareli
Vastra Kosh
Venilal Saris/ Venilal's
Vikram Phadnis
W
Warp 'n' Weft

CASUAL - WESTERN

Abraham & Thakore
Adidas
Aftershock
AND Designs/ Anita Dongre
Apparel Store
Araiya
Bar Code
Barefoot
Be:
Blackberrys
Body Sport
Chai
Charagh Din
Chemistry
Christina
Clothes Rack
Color Plus
Cotton Lollypop
Cotton World Corp
Cottons (Jaipur)
Cypress
Energy
Eternia
Fabindia
Finlay's
Gabbana
H. Couture
Hangten
Hum India
Indian States
In - Urges
Ixtapa
J'aime
JVP
Karma Kola
Kaysons
Kink
Lacoste
Lee
Levi's
Live-in Store
Madame
Malabar Boutique
Mango/ MNG
Marks & Spencer

Mélange
Mogra
Moksh
Morgan
MTV Factory
Outlet
Naina's
Natalzee
Neeta Lulla
Nike
Nimesis
NU
Ofran
On My Own (OMO)
Oobe
Orange Plum
Originals Unlimited!
Oz
Pagli
Pepe
Peppertree
Phat Fish
Planet Sports
Potion 9
Pramanik
Provogue
Provogue Lounge
Q!
Ragz Genes
Reebok
Remanika
Revolution
Rock Fashion Studio
Rockport
Roots
Rouge
Salim Asgarally
Selection Centre
Shakun
Sheetal
Sheetal Design Studio
Si Branché
Sign O' Times
Soshé
Spykar Jeans
Studio F
Studio Prêt
Studio Sinitta
Style Mantra
Tango
Tent
The Loot
The Oak Tree
The SF Jeans Company
Tirawa
Tommy Hilfiger
Tonyland
Trigger
Turquoise
Uni Style Image
United Colors of
Benetton
Weekender
What?
What's Pink
Wills Lifestyle
Woodland
Wrangler
X'Mex Clothing
You
Zooni

CLUB WEAR

Aftershock
Ananya
Araiya
Barefoot
Be:
Boulevard Benzer/
Rocky S Jeans
Chai
Cypress
Designs Unlimited
Galleria
High
Himation
In - Urges
Istante
Ixtapa
J'aime
JVP
Karma Kola
Kink
Mango/ MNG
Manish Arora/ Fish Fry
Morgan
Nagma's
Natalzee
Nimesis
NU
Ofran
Oz
Phat Fish
Potion 9
Provogue Lounge
Q!
Remanika
Rink's
Rock Fashion Studio
Roots
Rouge
Salim Asgarally
Si Branché
Sign O' Times
Soshé
Studio Sinitta
Style Mantra
Tent
The Oak Tree
Tirawa
What?
What's Pink
X'Mex Clothing
You
Zinc
7 BEST Marg

EXECUTIVE WEAR

Amber and Shirrin
Ashish N Soni
Bar Code
Chai
Charagh Din
Color Plus
Energy
Fabindia
Istaa
Mango/ MNG
Marks & Spencer
Narendra Kumar
NU
Ofran
Oobe
Provogue
Provogue Lounge
Shruti
The Double Bull
Wagon
Tulsi
United Colors of
Benetton
W
Wills Lifestyle

FORMAL - INDIAN

Aadi's
Aari
Abu Jani & Sandeep
Khosla
Adarsh Gill
Amâya
Amber and Shirrin
AND Designs/ Anita
Dongre
Antè Body
Araiya
Archana Kocchar
Arjun Khanna
Azeem Khan
Be:
Benu Sehgall Originals
Biba
Boulevard Benzer/
Rocky S Jeans
Brahma Selections
Burlingtons of Bombay
Christina
Cypress
Dadar Emporium

FORMAL - WESTERN

HANDBAGS & LEATHER GOODS

Joy Shoes
Karma Kola
Kink
Leather Farm
Leather Touch
Louis Vuitton
Maheka Mirpuri/ IV Fashion Life
Malabar Boutique
Mango/ MNG
Marks & Spencer
Mélange
Metro
Mogra
Moksh
Mont Blanc
Morgan
Moss
Nagma's
Natalzee
Nimesis
Nine West
NU
Ofran
On My Own (OMO)
Oz
Pagli
Phat Fish
Potion 9
Q!
Rasulbhai Adamji
Remanika
Rinaldi Designs
Ritu Kumar
Rock Fashion Studio
Roma
Romance
Roots
Rouge
Royal Leather
Salim Asgarally
Sambena
Samsonite
Scandal
Shlok
Si Branché
Soshé
Style Mantra
Sun - Way Leather House
Swarovski
Tarun Tahiliani
Tent
The Oak Tree
Tirawa
Tommy Hilfiger
Tulsi
United Colors of Benetton
Urvee's
What?
What's Pink
Wills Lifestyle
X'Mex Clothing
Zinc
7 BEST Marg

IMITATION JEWELLERY

Aadi's
Aakanksha
Aftershock
Aigner
Amber and Shirrin
Amrapali Jewels
Ananya
Araiya
Barefoot
Beauti Art
Choksi
Cottons (Jaipur)
Culture Shop
Curio Cottage
Cypress
Dee Jay
Estelle
Eternia
Fuel
Golden Thimble
High
In - Urges
Ishna
Istaa
Istante
Jewelart
Joolry
Karma Kola
Lady Grace
Le Bijou
Maheka Mirpuri/ IV Fashion Life
Malabar Boutique
Mango/ MNG
Mogra
Moksh
Morgan
Nagma's
Natalzee
NU
Ofran
On My Own (OMO)
Peppertree
Phat Fish
Potion 9
Reia
Remanika
Rock Fashion Studio
Romance
Roots
Rouge
Sheetal
Shehenaz
Shlok
Si Branché
Sia
Silver Age
Soshé
Swarovski
Tent
The Jewellery Plaza
The Oak Tree
Tiptop Point
Urvee's
Vaishali
Zinc

LINGERIE & NIGHTWEAR

Apparel Store
Eternia
Finlay's
Hum India
Le Bijou
Marks & Spencer
Only Woman
Open Secrets & Lifestyles
Pagli
Passion Flower
Roots
Saundarya
SD Lounge
Sheetal
Sleep-ins
Studio Lingerie
Zinc

MATERNITY WEAR

Amâya
Apparel Store
Fabindia
Green Bell
Just Maternity
Me 'N' Moms

PLUS SIZES

AND Designs/ Anita Dongre
Bandhej
Bar Code
Cottons (Jaipur)
Christina
Energy
Fabindia
Nagma's
Revolution

Studio F
Turquoise
Zooni

RESORT WEAR

Ananya
Anokhi
Apparel Store
Barefoot
Cypress
Globus
Himation
Ixtapa
Mango/ MNG
Orange Plum
Phat Fish
Rouge
Shoppers' Stop
Si Branché
Studio Lingerie
Tent
The Oak Tree
United Colors of Benetton
Vāmā
Westside
Zinc

SHOES

Adidas
Aigner
Aldo
Azeem Khan
Bally
Barefoot
Bata
Be:
Body Basics
Body Sport
Bon Bon
Calzarre
Candy
Catwalk
Cheemo
Citywalk
Cypress
Empire
Fabindia
Faith
Fendy Shoes
Footsie
Frenzy
FuToes
Galleria
Golden Touch
Habit Shoes
Himation
Inc. 5
In XS
Ishna
Istante
Joy Shoes
Karma Kola
Kink
Krishna Mehta
Lord's
Mango/ MNG
Marks & Spencer
Metro
Moss
Nagma's
Nike
Nimesis
Nine West
Ofran
Oz
Pagli
Part 1 Accessories
Phat Fish
Planet Sports
Potion 9
Pretty Walk
Q!
Reebok
Regal
Revolutions
Rinaldi Designs
Rock Fashion Studio
Rockport
Salim Asgarally
Scandal
Selection Centre
Shlok
Si Branché
Skin Sin
Sole to Soul
Soshé
Style Mantra
Svago
Tarun Tahiliani
The Loft
The Loot
The Oak Tree
Tirawa
Tommy Hilfiger
Trends
Urvee's
What?
Woodland
X'Mex Clothing
Zinc
7 BEST Marg

WINTER WEAR

Apparel Store
Chemistry
Clothes Rack
Mango/ MNG
MTV Factory Outlet
Tommy Hilfiger
Uni Style Image
United Colors of Benetton

AREA-WISE INDEX

AREA WISE INDEX

CHURCHGATE, CHOWPATTY, MARINE DRIVE & OPERA HOUSE

Amâya
Anokhi
Arrow
Cheemo
Cottons (Jaipur)
Finlay's
Fuel
Lord & Taylor
Raymond's
Regal
Spykar Jeans
Sushobhit
Vaishali
Vareli
Venilal Saris/ Venilal's
Westside

COLABA & CUFFE PARADE

Abraham & Thakore
Adarsh Gill
Adidas
Allen Solly
Arrow
Ashish N Soni
Atmosphere
Azeem Khan
Bar Code
Bata
Burlingtons of Bombay
Cambridge
Canali
Central Cottage Industries
Charagh Din
Citywalk
Clothes Rack
Color Plus
Cotton World Corp
Cottons
Curio Cottage
Daks
Ego
Energy
Garden
Habit Shoes
Hakoba
Indigo Nation
Jaipur Bandhej
Joy Shoes
Kachins Clothing
Lacoste
Lee
Levi's
Lord's
Louis Vuitton
Malabar Boutique
Manish Arora/ Fish Fry
Master Pieces - Galerie de Designe
Metro
Mont Blanc
Moon River
Narendra Kumar
Nike
Part 1 Accessories
Pepe
Pratap
Q!
Rabani & Rakha
Radhika Naik
Rasulbhai Adamji
Ravissant
Raymond's
Red Blue & Yellow
Rinaldi Designs
Rohit Bal
Roma
Sambena
Shilpa K
Sidewalks of the World
Street Market
Studio F
Suneet Varma
Tarun Tahiliani
The Courtyard
The Double Bull Wagon
The Indian Textiles Company
The Oak Tree
Tommy Hilfiger
Tulsi
Turquoise
United Colors of Benetton
Urban Wear
W
Wills Lifestyle
Woodland
Wrangler
Yamini
Zodiac
7 BEST Marg

CRAWFORD MARKET & BYCULLA

Citywalk
Indigo Nation
Lord's
Man O' Man
Metro
Reid & Taylor
Roma
Roopam
Sheetal
Street Market
The Juniors Shoppe
Zodiac

DADAR

Adidas
Babubhai Bhavanji
Bata
Cambridge
Cottons
Dadar Emporium
Empire
Garden
Indigo Nation
Lāzāree
Metro
Paaneri
Rangoli
Raymond's
Roop Milan
Roop Sangam
Wrangler

FORT & KALAGHODA

Akbarally's
Arrow
Bata
Ensemble
Fabindia
Fila and Proline
Gini & Jony
Golden Thimble
Lee
Raymond's
Reid & Taylor
Samsonite
Selection Centre
Street Market
The Bombay Stores
Trouser Town
Westside
Yantra
Zodiac

GOREGAON

Allen Solly
Arjun Khanna
Bata
Color Plus
Cotton Lollypop
Lawman
Pagli

GRANT ROAD, HAJI ALI & TARDEO

AND Designs/ Anita Dongre
Bata
Cambridge
Catwalk
Color Plus
Designs Unlimited
Ermenegildo Zegna
Floral
Freelook
Joolry
Lacoste
Lord's
Mango/ MNG
Marco
Marks & Spencer
Metro
Morgan
Ofran
Open Secrets & Lifestyles
Palate
Pantaloons
Pepe
Peppertree
Piramyd
Pitambari
Planet Fashion
Planet Sports
Provogue
Red Blue & Yellow
Ritu Kumar
Rouge
Ruff Kids'
Samsonite
Satya Paul
Sheetal Design Studio
Sleep-ins
Spykar Jeans
Swarovski
Uni Style Image
United Colors of Benetton

JUHU & SANTACRUZ

Aigner
Allen Solly
Bally
Bandhej
Bata
Boulevard Benzer/ Rocky S Jeans
Cambridge
Catwalk
Chic Baby
Christina
Cotton World Corp
De Hauz Khas
Galleria
Gold Leaf
Golden Thimble
Hidesign
Istante
Ixtapa
Jaipur Saree Kendra
Jane Shilton
Kala Niketan
Kaysons
Kimaya
Men's Boulevard
Millionaire
Neeta Lulla
Nisha Sagar
Paraphernalia
Passion Flower
Payal Singhal
Pitambari
Puravi Modgil
Rahul Agasti
Raymond's
Regal
Reid & Taylor
Ritu Kumar
Royal Leather
Sakhi
Samsonite
Satya Paul
Shyam Ahuja
Sia
Skin Sin
Soshé
The Bombay Stores
Trésorie
United Colors of Benetton
Vaishali
Vikram Phadnis
What?
Zedds
Zodiac

KALBADEVI & BHULESHWAR

Abhushan
Bata
Bhakti Creations
Cambridge
Chor Bazaar
James Ferriera
Lady Grace
New Pink Lady
Raj Kamal Sarees
Reshma
Street Markets
Tiptop Point
Venilal Saris/ Venilal's

KEMPS CORNER & CUMBALA HILL

AND Designs/ Anita Dongre
Antè Body
Apparel Store
Bambino
Bata
Be:
Biba
Candy
Catwalk
Empire
Energy
Faith
Footsie
Frenzy
FuToes
Good Earth
Habit Shoes
Hidesign
Himation
Images
In - Urges
IN XS
Kittens
Lladro
Millionaire
Planet Fashion
Ravissant
Remanika
Sajid Design Studio
Sambena
Samsonite
Shakun
Shringar
Sia
Studio Sajid
Style Mantra
Telon
Trends
You

KHAR

Abracadabra
Adidas
Arrow
Bata
Blackberrys
Bon Bon
Clothes Rack
Cypress
Dockers
File and Proline
Gabbana
Gini & Jony

Hum India
J'aime
Karma Kola
KBN
Lee
Levi's
Moss
Nike
Reebok
Revolution
Sagar
Salim Asgarally
Samsonite
Scram
S'warya
The Loot
Tusçan Verve
Woodland
Zinc

LOWER PAREL & PRABHADEVI

Adidas
Aldo
Amber and Shirrin
AND Designs/ Anita Dongre
Bandhej
Bata
Be:
Benu Sehgall Originals
Blackberry
Boulevard Benzer/ Rocky S Jeans
Calzarre
Chai
Colorplus
Gini & Jony
Good Earth
Hangten
Hurley's
Inc 5
Jane Shilton
JVP
Kaysons
Krishna Mehta
L'vista
Lacoste
Levi's
Lifestyle
Maheka Mirpuri/ IV Fashion Life
Marks & Spencer
ME - Furniture & Beyond
Metro
Mogra
Mykraft
Nike
Oobç
Pantaloons
Pepe
Pinakin
Provogue Lounge
Remanika
Ritu Kumar
Samsonite
Shlok
Spykar Jeans
Studio Lingerie
The Loot
The SF Jeans Company
Weekender
Wrangler

MALABAR HILL & NAPEAN SEA ROAD

Aari
Abu Jani & Sandeep Khosla
Ajay Anand
Brahma Selection
Contemporary Arts & Crafts
H. Couture
Instyle
Jaipur Bandhej
Jaipur Saree Kendra
Kamdhenu
Lee
Originals Unlimited!
Peacock Forever
Reshma
Roots
Shruti
Urvee's
Vaishali
Vandana Creation
Vividha
Yantra
Zodiac

MALAD & BORIVALI

Barbie
Bata
Biba
Blackberrys
Catwalk
Fabindia
Freelook
Gini & Jony
Intouch Leather
Lifestyle
Lilliput
Marco Ricci
Marks & Spencer
Men's Boulevard
Metro
Oobç
Rainbow
Raymond's
Regal
Reia
Revolutions
Ritu Kumar
Rockport
Samsonite
Scram
SD Lounge
Shoppers' Stop
Sia
United Colors of Benetton
Vaishali
W
Wills Lifestyle

MARINE LINES & DHOBI TALAO

Body Sport
Caxton Sports
India Emporium
Indian States
Kala Niketan
Levi's
Mayuri
MTV Factory Outlet
Nike
Queens Emporium
Roop Milan
Spykar Jeans
Star Sports
The Champion Sports
The Loot
Urvashi
Vanzasons
Warp 'n' Weft

MATUNGA

Bata
Clothes Rack
Milap
Pramanik
Romance
Sia

MULUND

Aadi's
Bata
Beauti Art
Cotton World Corp.
Cottons
Dee Jay
Green World
Kittens

Lifestyle
Lilliput
Live-in Store
Mykraft
Nike
Only Woman
Pretty Walk
Purple Kids
Raymond's
Reia
Remanika
Roman Park
Ruff Kids
Samsonite
Shoppers' Stop
Trigger
Weekender
Westside

NARIMAN POINT

Aftershock
Amrapali Jewels
Biba
Calzarre
Catwalk
Cheemo
Chemistry
Christina
Faith
Fendy Shoes
FuToes
Golden Touch
Hidesign
Hugo Boss
Jolly
Kaysons
Lacoste
Leather Farm
Leather Touch
Ms. Banjaran
Ravissant
Raymond's
Regal
Revolutions
Ritu Kumar
Royal Leather
Shehenaz
Swarovski
Zodiac

PEDDAR ROAD & ALTAMOUNT ROAD

Araiya
Be:
Bungalow Eight
Cheemo
Just Maternity
Libas
Mélange
NU
Orange Plum
Paraphernalia
Payal Singhal
Priya & Chintan
Rui
Satya Paul
Shyam Ahuja
Studio Sinitta
Sun - Way Leather House
United Colors of Benetton
Vāmā

POWAI & VASHI

Bata
Culture Shop
Hakoba
Hangten
Jashn
Lilliput
Live-in Store
Oobç
Pantaloons
Pretty Walk
Purple Kids
Roop Sangam
Ruff Kids
Samsonite
Street Market
The Loft
The Loot
Weekender
4 2 14 Originals

THANE

Allen Solly
Pantaloons
Ruff Kids'
Shyam Ahuja
Zodiac

VILE PARLE

Aakanksha
Archana Kochhar
Bata
Clothes Rack
Green Bell
Kala Niketan
Mayuri
Me 'N' Moms
Men's Boulevard
Nike
Nimesis
Purple Kids
Reebok
The Jewellery Plaza

CLOTHING & SHOE SIZE CONVERSION CHART

CHILDREN'S FOOTWEAR

American	8	9	10	11	12	12	1	2	3
Continental	24	25	27	28	29	30	32	33	34
British / Indian	7	8	9	10	11	12	13	1	2

CHILDREN'S WEAR

American	3	4	5	6	6X
Continental	98	104	110	116	122
British / Indian	18	20	22	24	26

LADIES' FOOTWEAR

American	5	6	7	8	9	10
Continental	36	37	38	39	40	41
British / Indian	3.5	4.5	5.5	6.5	7.5	8.5

LADIES' SKIRTS & DRESSES

American	3	5	7	9	11	12	13	14	15
Continental	36	38	38	40	40	42	42	44	44
British / Indian	8	10	11	12	13	14	15	16	17

LADIES' TOPS

American	10	12	14	16	18	20
Continental	38	40	42	44	46	48
British / Indian	32	34	36	38	40	42

MEN'S FOOTWEAR

American	7	8	9	10	11	12	13
Continental	39.5	41	42	43	44.5	46	47
British / Indian	6	7	8	9	10	11	12

MEN'S SHIRTS

American	14	15	15.5	16	16.5	17	17.5	18
Continental	37	38	39	41	42	43	44	45
British / Indian	14	15	15.5	16	16	17	17.5	18

MEN'S SUITS

American	34	36	38	40	42	44	46	48
Continental	44	46	48	50	52	54	56	58
British / Indian	34	36	38	40	42	44	46	48

INDEX

MAPS

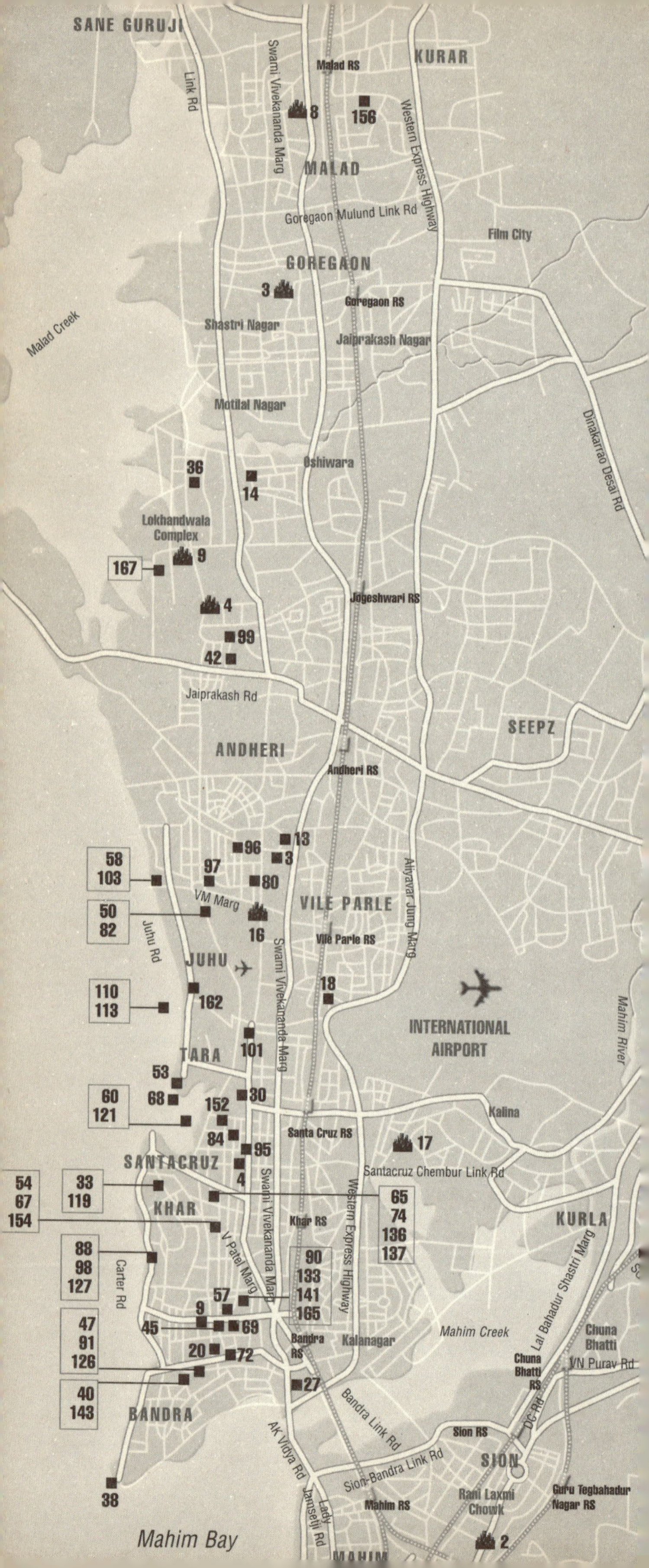
SANE GURUJI
KURAR
Malad RS
Link Rd
Swami Vivekananda Marg
Western Express Highway
8
156
MALAD
Goregaon Mulund Link Rd
Film City
GOREGAON
3
Goregaon RS
Malad Creek
Shastri Nagar
Jaiprakash Nagar
Motilal Nagar
Dinakarrao Desai Rd
Oshiwara
36
14
Lokhandwala Complex
9
167
4
Jogeshwari RS
99
42
Jaiprakash Rd
SEEPZ
ANDHERI
Andheri RS
13
96
3
58
103
97
80
VM Marg
50
82
16
VILE PARLE
Aliyavar Jung Marg
Juhu Rd
Vile Parle RS
JUHU
110
113
162
18
INTERNATIONAL AIRPORT
Mahim River
101
TARA
53
68
30
60
121
152
Kalina
84
Santa Cruz RS
95
17
SANTACRUZ
4
Santacruz Chembur Link Rd
54
67
154
33
119
KHAR
65
74
136
137
Khar RS
KURLA
88
98
127
Carter Rd
V Patel Marg
90
133
141
165
57
9
47
91
126
45
69
Mahim Creek
Chuna Bhatti
Lal Bahadur Shastri Marg
Bandra RS
Kalanagar
20
72
Chuna Bhatti RS
VN Purav Rd
40
143
27
Bandra Link Rd
BANDRA
AK Vidya Rd
Sion RS
DG Rd
SION
Sion-Bandra Link Rd
38
Jamsetji Rd
Lady
Mahim RS
Rani Laxmi Chowk
Guru Tegbahadur Nagar RS
Mahim Bay
2
MAHIM

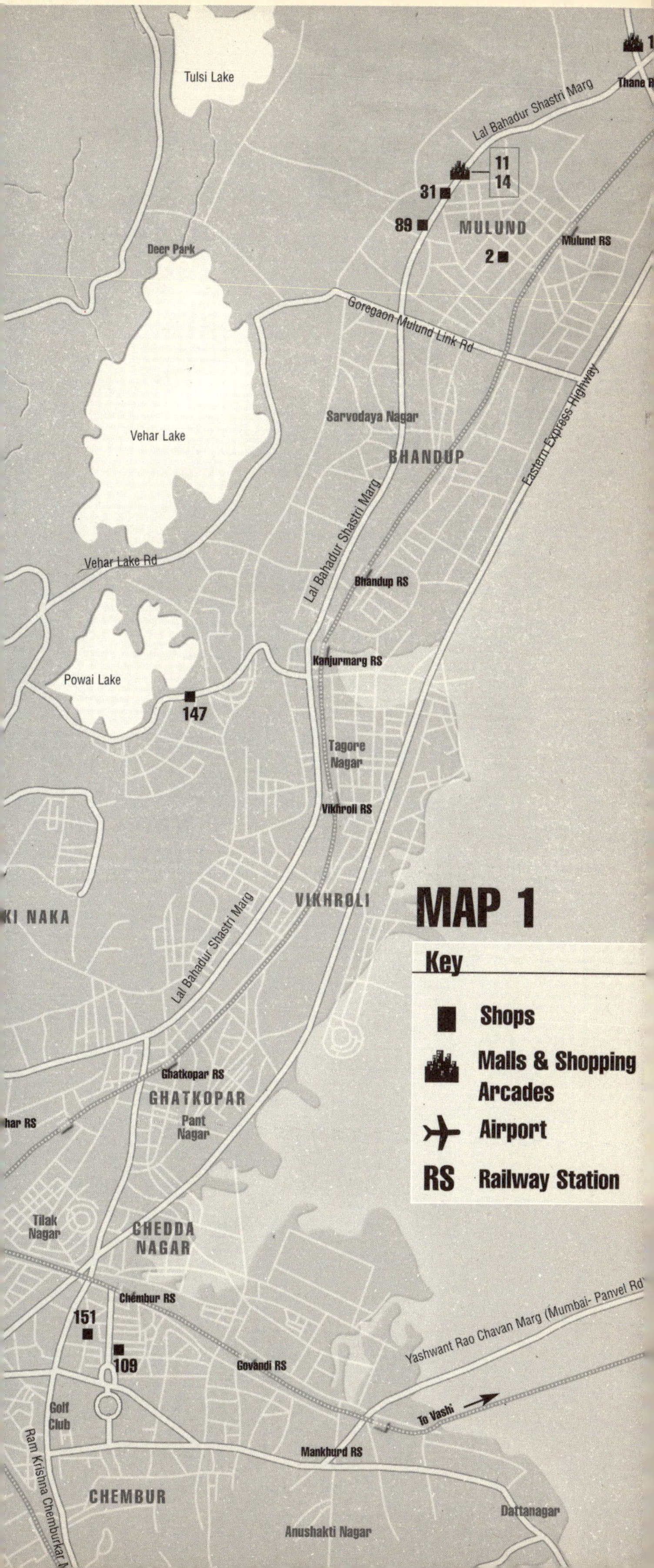

Tulsi Lake
Thane R
Lal Bahadur Shastri Marg
11
14
31
89
MULUND
2
Mulund RS
Deer Park
Goregaon Mulund Link Rd
Vehar Lake
Sarvodaya Nagar
BHANDUP
Eastern Express Highway
Lal Bahadur Shastri Marg
Vehar Lake Rd
Bhandup RS
Kanjurmarg RS
Powai Lake
147
Tagore Nagar
Vikhroli RS
VIKHROLI
KI NAKA
Lal Bahadur Shastri Marg
MAP 1
Key
Shops
Malls & Shopping Arcades
Airport
RS Railway Station
Ghatkopar RS
GHATKOPAR
Pant Nagar
har RS
Tilak Nagar
CHEDDA NAGAR
Chembur RS
151
109
Yashwant Rao Chavan Marg (Mumbai- Panvel Rd)
Govandi RS
Golf Club
To Vashi
Mankhurd RS
Ram Krishna Chemburkar M
CHEMBUR
Dattanagar
Anushakti Nagar

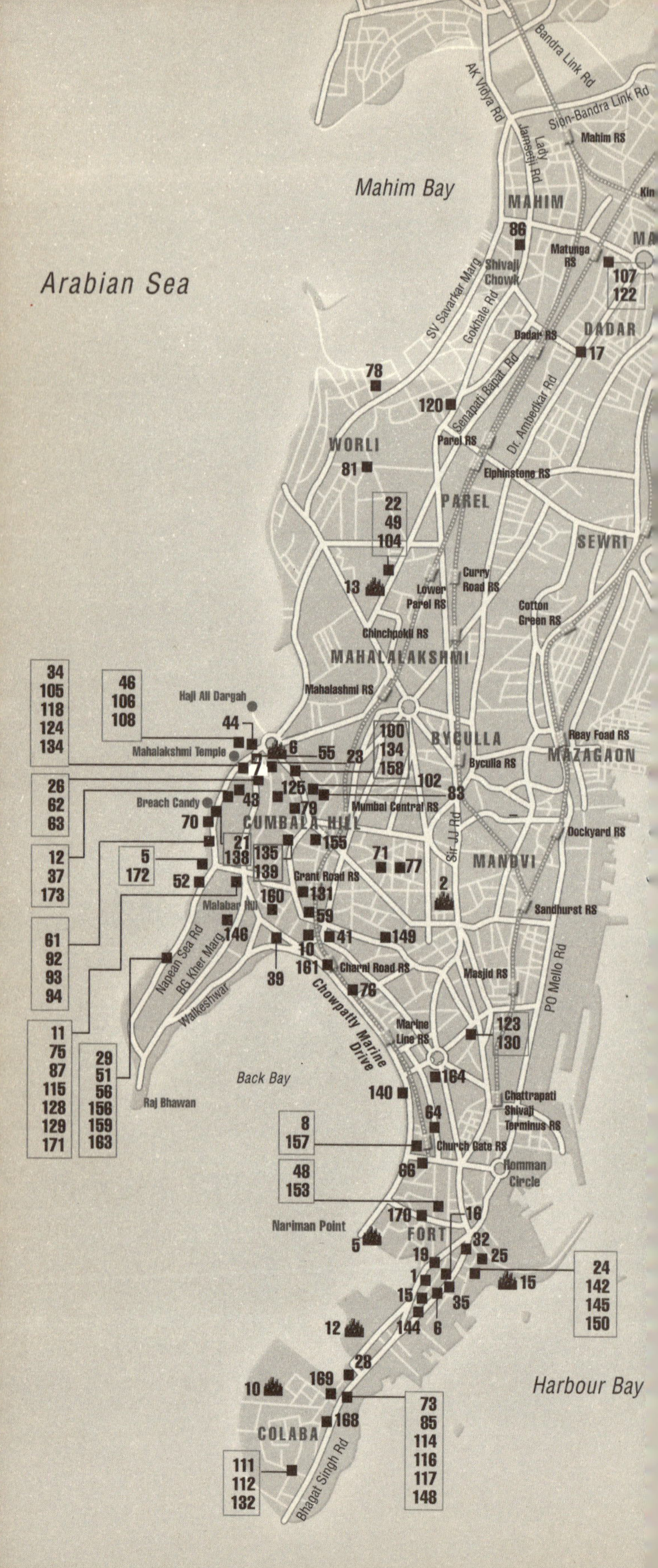
Arabian Sea
Mahim Bay
Back Bay
Harbour Bay
Bandra Link Rd
Sion-Bandra Link Rd
AK Vidya Rd
Lady Jamsetji Rd
Mahim RS
MAHIM
Matunga RS
Shivaji Chowk
SV Savarkar Marg
Gokhale Rd
Dadar RS
DADAR
Senapati Bapat Rd
Dr. Ambedkar Rd
WORLI
Parel RS
Elphinstone RS
PAREL
SEWRI
Curry Road RS
Lower Parel RS
Cotton Green RS
Chinchpokli RS
MAHALALAKSHMI
Mahalashmi RS
Haji Ali Dargah
Mahalakshmi Temple
BYCULLA
Byculla RS
Reay Road RS
MAZAGAON
Breach Candy
Mumbai Central RS
CUMBALA HILL
Dockyard RS
Sir JJ Rd
MANDVI
Grant Road RS
Malabar Hill
Sandhurst RS
Napean Sea Rd
BG Kher Marg
Charni Road RS
Walkeshwar
Chowpatty Marine Drive
Masjid RS
PO Mello Rd
Marine Line RS
Raj Bhawan
Chattrapati Shivaji Terminus RS
Church Gate RS
Romman Circle
Nariman Point
FORT
COLABA
Bhagat Singh Rd

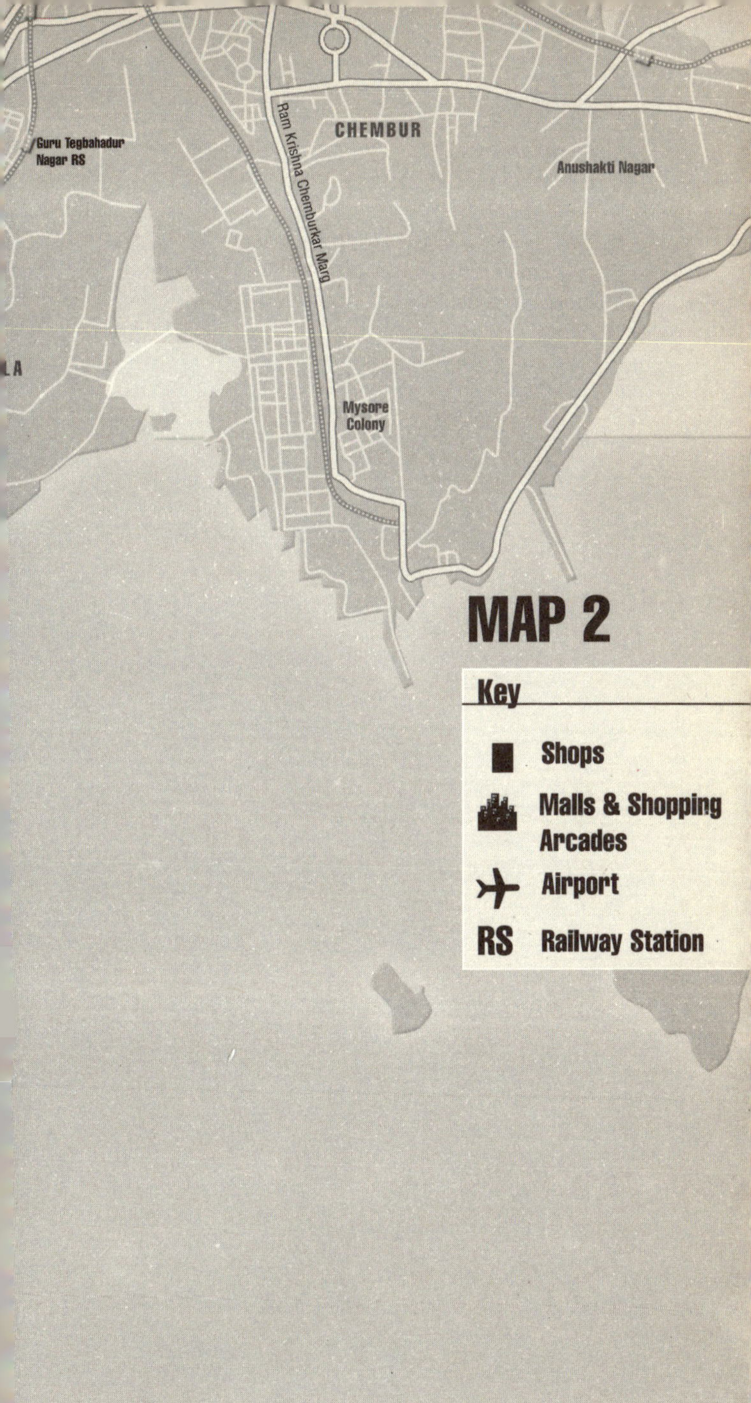

MAP 2

Key

- Shops
- Malls & Shopping Arcades
- Airport
- RS Railway Station

MAP KEY

Map No.		Shop Name	Page No.
MAP2	111	Q!	92
MAP2	112	Radhika Naik	93
MAP1	113	Rahul Agasti	94
MAP2	114	Rasulbhai Adamji	95
MAP2	115	Ravissant	95
MAP2	116	Raymond's	95
MAP2	117	Red Blue & Yellow	96
MAP2	118	Remanika	97
MAP1	119	Revolution	98
MAP2	120	Rinaldi Designs	98
MAP1	121	Ritu Kumar	76
MAP2	122	Romance	100
MAP2	123	Roopam	101
MAP2	124	Roots	101
MAP2	125	Rouge	102
MAP1	126	Ruff Kids	102
MAP1	127	Salim Asgarally	104
MAP2	128	Sambena	104
MAP2	129	Satya Paul	105
MAP2	130	Sheetal	107
MAP2	131	Sheetal Design Studio	107
MAP2	132	Shilpa K	107
MAP1	133	Shoppers Stop	108
MAP2	134	Shyam Ahuja	109
MAP2	135	Sia	109
MAP1	136	Sole to Soul	111
MAP1	137	Studio M	113
MAP2	138	Style Mantra	114
MAP2	139	Sun- Way Leather House	114
MAP2	140	Sushobhit	114
MAP1	141	Swarovski	115
MAP2	142	Tarun Tahiliani	116
MAP1	143	Telon	116
MAP2	144	The Bombay Store	117
MAP2	145	The Indian Textiles Company	118
MAP2	146	The Juniors Shoppe	119
MAP1	147	The Loft	119
MAP2	148	The Oak Tree	119
MAP2	149	Tiptop Point	120
MAP2	150	Tommy Hilfiger	121
MAP1	151	Tonyland	121
MAP1	152	Trésorie	121
MAP2	153	Trouser Town	122
MAP1	154	Tuscan Verve	123
MAP2	155	United Colors of Benetton	123
MAP1	156	Vaishali	124
MAP2	157	Vāishali	124
MAP2	158	Vama	125
MAP2	159	Vandana Creation	125
MAP2	160	Vanzasons	125
MAP2	161	Venilal Saris/ Venilal's	126
MAP1	162	Vikram Phadnis	126
MAP2	163	Vividha	126
MAP2	164	Warp 'n' Weft	127
MAP1	165	Weekender	127
MAP2	166	Westside	128
MAP1	167	White Window	128
MAP2	168	Woodland	129
MAP2	169	Yamini	130
MAP2	170	Yantra	130
MAP2	171	You	130
MAP2	172	Zodiac	131
MAP2	173	Zooni	131

MALLS & SHOPPING ARCADES

Map No.	Shop Name
1.	Amrapali Shopping Centre
2.	Chor Bazaar
3.	Citi Centre
4.	Citi Mall
5.	CR2
6.	Crossroads
7.	Heera Panna Shopping Arcade
8.	Inorbit Mall
9.	Lokhandwala Complex
10.	Maker Arcade
11.	Nirmal Lifestyle Mall
12.	Oberoi Shopping Arcade
13.	Phoenix Mills
14.	R Mall
15.	Taj Mahal Hotel
16.	Vaishali Shopping Centre
17.	Grand Hyatt Plaza